Anson D. F Randolph

**A Handy Book of Old and Familiar Hymns**

Anson D. F Randolph

**A Handy Book of Old and Familiar Hymns**

ISBN/EAN: 9783744779258

Printed in Europe, USA, Canada, Australia, Japan

Cover: Foto ©Thomas Meinert / pixelio.de

More available books at **www.hansebooks.com**

# A HANDY BOOK

### OF

# Old and Familiar Hymns

COMPILED BY

THE EDITOR OF "THE CHANGED CROSS," ETC.

ANSON D
900

COPYRIGHT 1883, BY
ANSON D. F. RANDOLPH & COMPANY.

# NOTE.

*It is not to be expected that a compilation within the limits of the present volume would contain* ALL *the Old and Familiar Hymns. The compiler has aimed in the selection to present the varied phases of ordinary Christian experience, in the belief, as has been well said by another, that next to Holy Scripture there is nothing that goes deeper, or expresses more clearly the condition and desires of the soul, than the Hymns and Songs of the Church.*

*The hymns marked* AB. *(abridged) are thus printed to preserve the forms in which they have long been commonly used, but the reader will find, as in the familiar hymns 'Jesus, I my cross have taken,' 'O Sacred*

*Head now wounded,' and others, that verses usually omitted in the Hymnals have been restored. No condensations, or changes in the text, have been attempted by the compiler, and the hymns, with the exceptions named, are printed in full, as this volume is not designed for use in public worship, but solely for devotional reading.*

# Old and Familiar Hymns.

### A SAFE STRONGHOLD.

A safe stronghold our God is still,
  A trusty shield and weapon;
He'll help us clear from all the ill
  That hath us now o'ertaken.
    The ancient Prince of hell
    Hath risen with purpose fell;
    Strong mail of craft and power
    He weareth in this hour,
On earth is not his fellow.

With force of arms we nothing can,
  Full soon were we down-ridden;
But for us fights the proper Man,
  Whom God Himself hath bidden.
    Ask ye, who is this same?
    Christ Jesus is His name,
    The Lord Sabaoth's Son,
    He and no other one
Shall conquer in the battle.

And were this world all devils o'er,
   And watching to devour us,
We lay it not to heart so sore,
   Not they can overpower us.
      And let the Prince of ill
      Look grim as e'er he will,
      He harms us not a whit:
      For why?   His doom is writ,
One little word shall slay him.

That word, for all their craft and force,
   One moment will not linger,
But, spite of hell, shall have its course,
   'Tis written by His finger.
      And though they take our life,
      Goods, honor, children, wife,
      Yet is their profit small;
      These things shall vanish all,
The Kingdom ours remaineth.

*Martin Luther.*<br>*Tr. by Thomas Carlyle.  st. alt.*

---

## OUR GOD, OUR HELP.

Our God, our help in ages past,
   Our hope for years to come;
Our shelter from the stormy blast,
   And our eternal home:

Under the shadow of Thy throne
    Thy saints have dwelt secure;
Sufficient is Thine arm alone,
    And our defence is sure.

Before the hills in order stood,
    Or earth received her frame,
From everlasting Thou art God,
    To endless years the same.

A thousand ages, in Thy sight,
    Are like an evening gone;
Short as the watch that ends the night,
    Before the rising sun.

Time, like an ever-rolling stream,
    Bears all its sons away;
They fly, forgotten, as a dream
    Dies at the opening day.

Our God, our help in ages past,
    Our hope for years to come,
Be Thou our guard while troubles last,
    And our eternal home.

*Rev. Isaac Watts. ab.*

---

## GOD MOVES IN A MYSTERIOUS WAY.

God moves in a mysterious way
    His wonders to perform;
He plants His footsteps in the sea,
    And rides upon the storm.

Deep in unfathomable mines
  Of never-failing skill,
He treasures up His bright designs,
  And works His sovereign will.

Ye fearful saints, fresh courage take;
  The clouds ye so much dread
Are big with mercy, and shall break
  In blessings on your head.

Judge not the Lord by feeble sense,
  But trust Him for His grace;
Behind a frowning providence
  He hides a smiling face.

His purposes will ripen fast,
  Unfolding every hour;
The bud may have a bitter taste,
  But sweet will be the flower.

Blind unbelief is sure to err,
  And scan His work in vain:
God is His own Interpreter,
  And He will make it plain.

*William Cowper.*

## WHEN ALL THY MERCIES, O MY GOD.

When all Thy mercies, O my God,
  My rising soul surveys,
Transported with the view, I'm lost
  In wonder, love, and praise.

## When all Thy Mercies.

O how shall words with equal warmth
  The gratitude declare
That glows within my ravished heart?
  But Thou canst read it there.

Unnumbered comforts to my soul
  Thy tender care bestowed,
Before my infant heart conceived
  From whom those comforts flowed.

When worn with sickness, oft hast Thou
  With health renewed my face;
And, when in sins and sorrows sunk,
  Revived my soul with grace.

Ten thousand thousand precious gifts
  My daily thanks employ;
Nor is the least a cheerful heart
  That tastes those gifts with joy.

Through every period of my life
  Thy goodness I'll pursue;
And after death, in distant worlds,
  The glorious theme renew.

Through all eternity to Thee
  A joyful song I'll raise;
For O, eternity's too short
  To utter all Thy praise.

*Joseph Addison.* ab

## HOW FIRM A FOUNDATION.

How firm a foundation, ye saints of the Lord,
Is laid for your faith in His excellent word!
What more can He say than to you He hath said,
You who unto Jesus for refuge have fled?

"Fear not, I am with thee, O be not dismayed,
For I am thy God, and will still give thee aid:
I'll strengthen thee, help thee, and cause thee to stand,
Upheld by My righteous, omnipotent hand.

"When through the deep waters I call thee to go,
The rivers of woe shall not thee overflow;
For I will be with thee thy trouble to bless,
And sanctify to thee thy deepest distress.

"When through fiery trials thy pathway shall lie,
My grace all sufficient shall be thy supply:
The flame shall not hurt thee; I only design
Thy dross to consume, thy gold to refine.

"E'en down to old age, all My people shall prove,
My sovereign, eternal, unchangeable love;

And when hoary hairs shall their temples adorn,
Like lambs they shall still in My bosom be borne.

"The soul that on Jesus hath leaned for repose
I will not, I will not desert to his foes;
That soul, though all hell should endeavor to shake,
I'll never, no never, no never forsake."

*George Keith. ab.*

---

## AS PANTS THE HART.

As pants the hart for cooling streams,
    When heated in the chase,
So longs my soul, O God, for Thee,
    And Thy refreshing grace.

For Thee, my God, the living God,
    My thirsty soul doth pine:
O when shall I behold Thy face,
    Thou Majesty Divine?

Why restless, why cast down, my soul?
    Trust God; Who will employ
His aid for thee, and change those sighs
    To thankful hymns of joy.

God of my strength, how long shall I
  Like one forgotten, mourn,
Forlorn, forsaken, and exposed
  To my oppressor's scorn.

My heart is pierced, as with a sword,
  While thus my foes upbraid:
"Vain boaster, where is now thy God?
  And where His promised aid?"

Why restless, why cast down, my soul?
  Trust God, and thou shalt sing
His praise again, and find Him still
  Thy health's eternal spring.
                    *Tate and Brady.*

---

### HOLY, HOLY, HOLY!

Holy, holy, holy! Lord God Almighty,
  Early in the morning our songs shall rise to Thee;
Holy, holy, holy! Merciful and Mighty!
  God in Three Persons, Blessed Trinity!

Holy, holy, holy! all the saints adore Thee,
  Casting down their golden crowns around the glassy sea;
Cherubim and Seraphim falling down before Thee,
  Which wert, and art, and evermore shall be.

*O Lord, how happy.*

Holy, holy, holy! though the darkness hide
    Thee,
  Though the eye of sinful man Thy glory
    may not see,
Only Thou art holy, there is none beside
    Thee,
  Perfect in power, in love and purity.

Holy, holy, holy! Lord God Almighty,
  All Thy works shall praise Thy name, in
    earth and sky and sea;
Holy, holy, holy! Lord God Almighty,
  God in Three Persons, Blessed Trinity!
        *Bp. Reginald Heber.*

## O LORD, HOW HAPPY.

O Lord, how happy should we be
If we could cast our care on Thee,
  If we from self could rest;
And feel at heart that One above
In perfect wisdom, perfect love,
  Is working for the best.

How far from this our daily life,
How oft disturbed by anxious strife,
  By sudden wilds alarms;
O could we but relinquish all
Our earthly props, and simply fall
  On Thine almighty arms!

Could we but kneel and cast our load,
E'en while we pray, upon our God,
 Then rise with lightened cheer;
Sure that the Father Who is nigh
To still the famished raven's cry,
 Will hear in that we fear.

We cannot trust Him as we should;
So chafes weak nature's restless mood
 To cast its peace away;
But birds and flowerets round us preach,
All, all the present evil teach
 Sufficient for the day.

Lord, make these faithless hearts of ours
Such lessons learn from birds and flowers;
 Make them from self to cease,
Leave all things to a Father's will,
And taste, before Him lying still,
 E'en in affliction. peace.
*Prof. Joseph Anstice.*

---

### WITH BROKEN HEART.

With broken heart and contrite sigh,
A trembling sinner, Lord, I cry:
Thy pardoning grace is rich and free;
O God, be merciful to me.

I smite upon my troubled breast,
With deep and conscious guilt opprest,

Christ and His cross my only plea;
O God, be merciful to me.

Far off I stand with tearful eyes,
Nor dare uplift them to the skies;
But Thou dost all my anguish see;
O God, be merciful to me.

Nor alms, nor deeds that I have done,
Can for a single sin atone;
To Calvary alone I flee;
O God, be merciful to me.

And when, redeemed from sin and hell,
With all the ransomed throng I dwell,
My raptured song shall ever be,
God has been merciful to me.
*Rev. Cornelius Elven.*

## GUIDE ME, O GREAT JEHOVAH.

Guide me, O Thou Great Jehovah,
   Pilgrim through this barren land;
I am weak, but Thou art mighty,
   Hold me with Thy powerful hand;
     Bread of heaven,
Feed me now and evermore.

Open now the crystal Fountain,
   Whence the healing streams do flow;

Let the fiery cloudy pillar
  Lead me all my journey through;
    Strong Deliverer,
Be Thou still my Strength and Shield.

When I tread the verge of Jordan,
  Bid my anxious fears subside:
Death of death, and hell's Destruction,
  Land me safe on Canaan's side;
    Songs of praises
I will ever give to Thee.

*Rev. William Williams.* ab.

---

## O DAY OF REST

O day of rest and gladness,
  O day of joy and light,
O balm of care and sadness,
  Most beautiful, most bright;
On thee the high and lowly
  Before th' eternal Throne
Sing Holy, Holy, Holy,
  To the great Three in One.

On thee, at the creation,
  The light first had its birth;
On thee for our salvation
  Christ rose from depths of earth;
On thee our Lord victorious
  The Spirit sent from heaven;
And thus on thee most glorious
  A triple light was given.

## O Day of Rest.

Thou art a cooling fountain
   In life's dry dreary sand;
From thee, like Pisgah's mountain,
   We view our promised land;
A day of sweet refection,
   A day of holy love,
A day of resurrection
   From earth to things above.

To-day on weary nations
   The heavenly Manna falls,
To holy convocations
   The silver trumpet calls,
Where Gospel light is glowing
   With pure and radiant beams,
And living water flowing
   With soul-refreshing streams.

New graces ever gaining
   From this our day of rest,
We reach the Rest remaining
   To spirits of the blest;
To Holy Ghost be praises,
   To Father, and to Son;
The Church her voice upraises
   To Thee, blest Three in One.

*Bp. Christopher Wordsworth*

## SAFELY, THROUGH ANOTHER WEEK

Safely, through another week,
   God has brought us on our way;
Let us now a blessing seek,
   Waiting in His courts to-day:
Day of all the week the best,
Emblem of eternal rest.

While we pray for pardoning grace,
   Through the dear Redeemer's name,
Show Thy reconcilèd face,
   Take away our sin and shame:
From our worldly cares set free,
May we rest this day in Thee.

Here we come Thy name to praise;
   May we feel Thy presence near:
May Thy glory meet our eyes,
   While we in Thy house appear:
Here afford us, Lord, a taste
Of our everlasting feast.

May Thy gospel's joyful sound
   Conquer sinners, comfort saints;
Make the fruits of grace abound,
   Bring relief for all complaints:
Thus may all our Sabbaths prove,
Till we join the Church above.

*Rev. John Newton*

## LO, ON A NARROW NECK OF LAND

Lo, on a narrow neck of land,
'Twixt two unbounded seas, I stand,
  Secure, insensible;
A point of time, a moment's space,
Removes me to that heavenly place,
  Or shuts me up in hell.

O God, mine inmost soul convert,
And deeply on my thoughtful heart
  Eternal things impress;
Give me to feel their solemn weight,
And tremble on the brink of fate,
  And wake to righteousness.

Before me place, in dread array,
The pomp of that tremendous day,
  When Thou with clouds shalt come
To judge the nations at Thy bar;
And tell me, Lord, shall I be there
  To meet a joyful doom?

Be this my one great business here,
With holy trembling, holy fear,
  To make my calling sure,
Thine utmost counsel to fulfil,
And suffer all Thy righteous will,
  And to the end endure.

Then, Saviour, then my soul receive,
Transported from this vale to live,
   And reign with Thee above,
Where faith is sweetly lost in sight,
And hope in full, supreme delight,
   And everlasting love.
     *Rev. Charles Wesley. ab. and alt.*

## THE VOICE OF FREE GRACE.

The voice of free grace cries, Escape to the mountain;
For Adam's lost race, Christ hath opened a fountain;
For sin, and uncleanness, and every transgression,
His blood flows most freely, in streams of salvation.
Hallelujah to the Lamb, who hath purchased our pardon,
We'll praise Him again, when we pass over Jordan.

Ye souls that are wounded, O flee to the Saviour;
He calls you in mercy, 'tis infinite favor;
Your sins are increaséd as high as a mountain.
His blood can remove them, it flows from the fountain,
    Hallelujah, etc.

Now Jesus, our King, reigns triumphantly glorious;
O'er sin, death, and hell, He is more than victorious;
With shouting proclaim it, O trust in His passion,
He saves us most freely, O glorious salvation!
      Hallelujah, etc.

With joy shall we stand, when escaped to the shore;
With harps in our hands, we will praise Him the more;
We'll range the sweet plains on the banks of the river,
And sing of salvation for ever and ever.
Hallelujah to the Lamb, who hath purchased our pardon,
We'll praise Him again, when we pass over Jordan.
      *Rev. Richard Burdsall. ab. and alt.*

---

## WHAT VARIOUS HINDRANCES.

What various hindrances we meet
In coming to the Mercy-seat;
Yet who, that knows the worth of prayer
But wishes to be often there?

## What various Hindrances.

Prayer makes the darkened cloud withdraw,
Prayer climbs the ladder Jacob saw,
Gives exercise to faith and love,
Brings every blessing from above.

Restraining prayer we cease to fight;
Prayer makes the Christian's armor bright;
And Satan trembles when he sees
The weakest saint upon his knees.

When Moses stood with arms spread wide,
Success was found on Israel's side;
But when through weariness they failed,
That moment Amalek prevailed.

Have we no words? ah, think again;
Words flow apace when we complain,
And fill our fellow-creature's ear
With the sad tale of all our care.

Were half the breath thus vainly spent
To heaven in supplication sent,
Our cheerful song would oftener be,
"Hear what the Lord hath done for me."

O Lord, increase our faith and love,
That we may all our goodness prove,
And gain from Thy exhaustless store
The fruits of prayer for evermore.

*William Cowper*

## COME, YE DISCONSOLATE.

Come, ye disconsolate, where'er ye languish,
Come to the mercy-seat, fervently kneel;
Here bring your wounded hearts, here tell your anguish,
Earth has no sorrows that heaven cannot heal.

Joy of the desolate, Light of the straying,
Hope of the penitent, fadeless and pure,
Here speaks the Comforter, tenderly saying,
Earth has no sorrows that heaven cannot cure.

Here see the Bread of Life; see waters flowing
Forth from the throne of God, pure from above;
Come to the feast prepared, come, ever knowing
Earth has no sorrows but heaven can remove.

*Thomas Moore. v, 1. 2. alt.*
*Thomas Hastings. v. 3.*

## RESTING FROM HIS WORK TO-DAY

Resting from His work to-day,
In the tomb the Saviour lay;
Still He slept, from head to feet
Shrouded in the winding-sheet,
Lying in the rock alone,
Hidden by the sealèd stone.

Late at even there was seen,
Watching long, the Magdalene;
Early, ere the break of day,
Sorrowful she took her way
To the holy garden glade,
Where her buried Lord was laid.

So with Thee, till life shall end,
I would solemn vigil spend;
Let me hew Thee, Lord, a shrine
In this rocky heart of mine,
Where, in pure embalmèd cell,
None but Thou may ever dwell.

Myrrh and spices will I bring,
True affection's offering;
Close the door from sight and sound
Of the busy world around;
And in patient watch remain
Till my Lord appear again.

*Rev. Thomas Whytehead.* ab

## LO, THE FEAST IS SPREAD TO-DAY!

Lo, the feast is spread to-day!
Jesus summons, come away!
From the vanity of life,
From the sounds of mirth and strife,
To the feast by Jesus given,
Come and taste the Bread of Heaven.

Why with proud excuse and vain,
Spurn His mercy once again?
From amidst life's social ties,
From the farm and merchandise,
Come, for all is now prepared;
Freely given, be freely shared.

Blessèd are the lips that taste
Our Redeemer's marriage feast;
Blessèd who on Him shall feed,
Bread of Life and drink indeed.
Blessèd, for their thirst is o'er,
They shall never hunger more.

Make, then, once again your choice,
Hear to-day His calling voice;
Servants, do your Master's will;
Bidden guests, His table fill;
Come, before His wrath shall swear:
Ye shall never enter there.

*Rev. Henry Alford.*

## WHILE THEE I SEEK.

While Thee I seek, protecting Power,
  Be my vain wishes stilled;
And may this consecrated hour
  With better hopes be filled.
Thy love the powers of thought bestowed
  To Thee my thoughts would soar;
Thy mercy o'er my life has flowed,
  That mercy I adore.

In each event of life, how clear
  Thy ruling hand I see:
Each blessing to my soul more dear,
  Because conferred by Thee.
In every joy that crowns my days,
  In every pain I bear,
My heart shall find delight in praise,
  Or seek relief in prayer.

When gladness wings my favored hour,
  Thy love my thoughts shall fill;
Resigned when storms of sorrow lower,
  My soul shall meet Thy will.
My lifted eye without a tear,
  The lowering storm shall see;
My steadfast heart shall know no fear,
  That heart will rest on Thee.
*Miss Helen Maria Williams*

## SWEET IS THE WORK.

Sweet is the work, my God, my King,
To praise Thy name, give thanks, and sing;
To show Thy love by morning light,
And talk of all Thy truth at night.

Sweet is the day of sacred rest;
No mortal cares shall seize my breast;
O may my heart in tune be found,
Like David's harp of solemn sound.

My heart shall triumph in my Lord,
And bless His works, and bless His word;
His works of grace, how bright they shine,
How deep His counsels, how divine.

Lord, I shall share a glorious part,
When grace hath well refined my heart,
And fresh supplies of joy are shed,
Like holy oil, to cheer my head.

Then shall I see, and hear, and know
All I desired or wished below;
And every power find sweet employ,
In that eternal world of joy.

*Rev. Isaac Watts. ab.*

## PRAISE, MY SOUL.

Praise, my soul, the King of Heaven;
   To His feet thy tribute bring;
Ransomed, healed, restored, forgiven,
   Evermore His praises sing:
     Alleluia! Alleluia!
   Praise the everlasting King.

Praise Him for His grace and favor
   To our fathers in distress;
Praise Him still the same as ever,
   Slow to chide, and swift to bless:
     Alleluia! Alleluia!
   Glorious in His faithfulness.

Father-like, He tends and spares us,
   Well our feeble frame He knows;
In His hands He gently bears us,
   Rescues us from all our foes:
     Alleluia! Alleluia!
   Praise with us the God of grace.

Angels in the height adore Him!
   Ye behold Him face to face:
Saints triumphant bow before Him!
   Gathered in of every race:
     Alleluia! Alleluia!
   Praise with us the God of grace.

*Rev. Henry Francis Lyte.*
*Rev. Sir Henry Williams Baker.*

## HOLY SPIRIT, LORD OF LIGHT.

Holy Spirit, Lord of light,
From Thy clear celestial height,
  Thy pure beaming radiance give.

Come, Thou Father of the poor,
Come, with treasures which endure,
  Come, Thou Light of all that live.

Thou, of all consolers best,
Visiting the troubled breast,
  Dost refreshing peace bestow.

Thou in toil art comfort sweet,
Pleasant coolness in the heat,
  Solace in the midst of woe.

Light immortal, Light divine,
Visit Thou these hearts of Thine,
  And our inmost being fill.

If Thou take Thy grace away,
Nothing pure in man will stay;
  All his good is turned to ill.

Heal our wounds, our strength renew,
On our dryness pour Thy dew;
  Wash the stains of guilt away.

Bend the stubborn heart and will,
Melt the frozen, warm the chill;
  Guide the steps that go astray.

Thou, on those who evermore
Thee confess and Thee adore,
  In Thy sevenfold gifts descend.

Give them comfort when they die,
Give them life with Thee on high;
  Give them joys which never end.
*Robert II., King of France.*<br>*Tr. by Rev. Edward Caswall.*

---

### COME, THOU FOUNT.

Come, thou Fount of every blessing,
  Tune my heart to sing Thy grace;
Streams of mercy never ceasing,
  Call for songs of loudest praise:
Teach me some melodious sonnet,
  Sung by flaming tongues above;
Praise the mount, I'm fixed upon it,
  Mount of God's unchanging love.

Here I raise my Ebenezer,
  Hither by Thy help I'm come;
And I hope, by Thy good pleasure,
  Safely to arrive at home:
Jesus sought me, when a stranger,
  Wandering from the fold of God;
He, to rescue me from danger,
  Interposed His precious blood.

O to grace how great a debtor,
   Daily I'm constrained to be:
Let that grace now, like a fetter,
   Bind my wandering heart to Thee:
Prone to wander, Lord, I feel it,
   Prone to leave the God I love;
Here's my heart, O take and seal it,
   Seal it from Thy courts above.

Rev. Robert Robinson.

---

## O MASTER, IT IS GOOD TO BE.

O Master, it is good to be
High on the mountain here with Thee;
Where stand revealed to mortal gaze
Those glorious saints of other days;
Who once received on Horeb's height
The eternal laws of truth and right;
Or caught the still small whisper, higher
Than storm, than earthquake, or than fire.

O Master, it is good to be
With Thee, and with Thy faithful Three;
Here, where the apostle's heart of rock
Is nerved against temptation's shock;
Here, where the son of thunder learns
The thought that breathes, and word that burns;
Here, where on eagle's wings we move
With Him whose last best creed is love.

O Master, it is good to be
Entranced, enwrapt, alone with Thee;
And watch Thy glistering raiment glow
Whiter than Hermon's whitest snow;
The human lineaments that shine
Irradiant with a light divine:
Till we too change from grace to grace,
Gazing on that transfigured Face.

O Master, it is good to be
Here on the holy mount with Thee:
When darkling in the depths of night,
When dazzled with excess of light,
We bow before the heavenly Voice
That bids bewildered souls rejoice,
Though love wax cold, and faith be dim,
"This is My Son, O hear ye Him."

*Rev. Arthur Penrhyn Stanley.*

---

## A CLOSER WALK WITH GOD.

O for a closer walk with God,
    A calm and heavenly frame!
A light to shine upon the road
    That leads me to the Lamb!

Where is the blessedness I knew
    When first I saw the Lord?
Where is the soul-refreshing view
    Of Jesus and His word?

What peaceful hours I once enjoyed!
   How sweet their memory still!
But they have left an aching void
   The world can never fill.

Return, O holy Dove! return,
   Sweet messenger of rest!
I hate the sins that made Thee mourn,
   And drove Thee from my breast.

The dearest idol I have known,
   Whate'er that idol be,
Help me to tear it from Thy throne,
   And worship only Thee!

So shall my walk be close with God,
   Calm and serene my frame;
So purer light shall mark the road
   That leads me to the Lamb.

*William Cowper*

---

## RISE, MY SOUL.

Rise, my soul, and stretch thy wings,
   Thy better portion trace;
Rise from transitory things
   Towards heaven, thy native place:
Sun and moon and stars decay;
   Time shall soon this earth remove;
Rise, my soul, and haste away
   To seats prepared above.

## Rise, my Soul.

Rivers to the ocean run,
    Nor stay in all their course;
Fire, ascending, seeks the sun;
    Both speed them to their source:
So a soul, that's born of God,
    Pants to view His glorious face,
Upward tends to His abode,
    To rest in His embrace.

Fly me, riches, fly me, cares,
    Whilst I that coast explore;
Flattering world, with all thy snares
    Solicit me no more!
Pilgrims fix not here their home;
    Strangers tarry but a night;
When the last dear morn is come,
    They'll rise to joyful light.

Cease, ye pilgrims, cease to mourn,
    Press onward to the prize;
Soon our Saviour will return
    Triumphant in the skies:
Yet a season, and you know
    Happy entrance will be given,
All our sorrows left below,
    And earth exchanged for heaven.

*Rev. Robert Seagrave. ab.*

## COME, HOLY SPIRIT.

Come, Holy Spirit, heavenly Dove,
    With all Thy quickening powers,
Kindle a flame of sacred love
    In these cold hearts of ours.

Look how we grovel here below,
    Fond of these trifling toys:
Our souls can neither fly nor go
    To reach eternal joys.

In vain we tune our formal songs,
    In vain we strive to rise;
Hosannas languish on our tongues,
    And our devotion dies.

Dear Lord, and shall we ever live
    At this poor dying rate,
Our love so faint, so cold to Thee,
    And Thine to us so great?

Come, Holy Spirit, heavenly Dove,
    With all Thy quickening powers,
Come, shed abroad a Saviour's love,
    And that shall kindle ours.

*Rev. Isaac Watts.*

## COME, MY SOUL, THY SUIT PREPARE.

Come, my soul, thy suit prepare,
Jesus loves to answer prayer;
He Himself has bid thee pray,
Therefore will not say thee nay.

Thou art coming to a King,
Large petitions with thee bring;
For His grace and power are such,
None can ever ask too much.

With my burden I begin,
Lord, remove this load of sin;
Let Thy blood, for sinners spilt,
Set my conscience free from guilt.

Lord, I come to Thee for rest,
Take possession of my breast;
There Thy blood-bought right maintain,
And without a rival reign.

While I am a pilgrim here,
Let Thy love my spirit cheer;
As my Guide, my Guard, my Friend,
Lead me to my journey's end.

Show me what I have to do,
Every hour my strength renew;
Let me live a life of faith,
Let me die Thy people's death.

*Rev. John Newton.  ab.*

## SINCE O'ER THY FOOTSTOOL.

Since o'er Thy footstool here below
   Such radiant gems are strewn,
Oh, what magnificence must glow,
   My God, about Thy throne!
So brilliant here those drops of light,—
There the full ocean rolls, how bright!

If night's blue curtain of the sky
   With thousand stars inwrought,
Hung like a royal canopy
   With glittering diamonds fraught,
Be, Lord, Thy temple's outer veil,
What splendor at the shrine must dwell!

The dazzling sun, at noontide hour,
   Forth from his flaming vase,
Flinging o'er earth the golden shower,
   Till vale and mountain blaze,
But shows, O Lord! one beam of Thine:
What, then, the day where Thou dost shine!

Ah! how shall these dim eyes endure
   That noon of living rays,
Or how my spirit so impure
   Upon Thy glory gaze?
Anoint, O Lord! anoint my sight,
And robe me for that world of light!
      *Rev. William Augustus Muhlenberg.*

## LEAD, KINDLY LIGHT.

Lead, kindly Light, amid the encircling gloom,
    Lead Thou me on;
The night is dark, and I am far from home;
    Lead Thou me on;
Keep Thou my feet; I do not ask to see
The distant scene; one step enough for me.

I was not ever thus, nor prayed that Thou
    Shouldst lead me on;
I loved to choose and see my path; but now
    Lead Thou me on!
I loved the garish day, and, spite of fears,
Pride ruled my will. Remember not past years!

So long Thy Power hast blest me, sure it still
    Will lead me on
O'er moor and fen, o'er crag and torrent, till
    The night is gone,
And with the morn those angel faces smile
Which I have loved long since, and lost awhile!

        *Rev. John Henry Newman.*

## WHEN I CAN READ MY TITLE.

When I can read my title clear
  To mansions in the skies,
I bid farewell to every fear,
  And wipe my weeping eyes.

Should earth against my soul engage,
  And hellish darts be hurled,
Then I can smile at Satan's rage,
  And face a frowning world.

Let cares like a wild deluge come,
  And storms of sorrow fall;
May I but safely reach my home,
  My God, my heaven, my all:

There shall I bathe my weary soul
  In seas of heavenly rest,
And not a wave of trouble roll
  Across my peaceful breast.
*Rev. Isaac Watts.*

---

## NEW EVERY MORNING.

New every morning is the love
Our wakening and uprising prove;
Through sleep and darkness safely brought,
Restored to life, and power, and thought.

New mercies, each returning day,
Hover round us while we pray;
New perils past, new sins forgiven,
New thoughts of God, new hopes of Heaven.

If on our daily course our mind
Be set to hallow all we find,
New treasures still, of countless price,
God will provide for sacrifice.

The trivial round, the common task,
Will furnish all we need to ask,
Room to deny ourselves, a road
To bring us daily nearer God.

Only, O Lord, in Thy dear love
Fit us for perfect rest above;
And help us, this and every day,
To live more nearly as we pray.
*Rev. John Keble.*

---

### AWAKE, MY SOUL.

Awake, my soul, and with the sun
Thy daily stage of duty run;
Shake off dull sloth, and joyful rise
To pay thy morning sacrifice.

Redeem thy mis-spent time that's past,
And live this day as if thy last;

## Awake, my Soul.

Improve thy talent with due care,
For the great day thyself prepare.

Let all thy converse be sincere,
Thy conscience as the noon-day clear;
Think how all-seeing God thy ways
And all thy secret thoughts surveys.

By influence of the light divine,
Let thy own light in good works shine;
Reflect all heaven's propitious rays
In ardent love and cheerful praise.

Wake, and lift up thyself, my heart,
And with the angels bear thy part,
Who, all night long, unwearied sing
High praise to Thee eternal King.

I wake, I wake, ye heavenly choir;
May your devotion me inspire;
That I like you my age may spend,
Like you may on my God attend.

All praise to Thee who safe hast kept,
And hast refreshed me whilst I slept;
Grant, Lord, when I from death shall wake,
I may of endless light partake.

Lord, I my vows to Thee renew;
Disperse my sins as morning dew;
Guard my first springs of thought and w
And with Thyself my spirit fill.

## Glory, my God, to Thee.

Direct, control, suggest this day,
All I design, or do, or say;
That all my powers, with all their might,
In Thy sole glory may unite.

Praise God, from whom all blessings flow;
Praise Him, all creatures here below;
Praise Him above, ye heavenly host;
Praise Father, Son, and Holy Ghost.

                    *Bp. Thomas Ken. ab.*

---

### GLORY, MY GOD, TO THEE.

Glory, my God, to Thee this night,
For all the blessings of the light;
Keep me, O keep me, King of kings,
Beneath Thine own almighty wings.

Forgive me, Lord, for Thy dear Son,
The ill that I this day have done;
That with the world, myself, and Thee,
I, ere I sleep, at peace may be.

Teach me to live, that I may dread
The grave as little as my bed;
To die, that this vile body may
Rise glorious at the awful day.

O may my soul on Thee repose,
And may sweet sleep my eyelids close;
Sleep, that shall me more vigorous make,
And serve my God when I awake.

When in the night I sleepless lie,
My soul with heavenly thoughts supply;
Let no ill dreams disturb my rest,
No powers of darkness me molest.

O, when shall I in endless day
Forever chase dark sleep away,
And hymns divine with angels sing,
Glory to Thee eternal King.

Praise God, from whom all blessings flow;
Praise Him, all creatures here below;
Praise Him above, ye heavenly host;
Praise Father, Son, and Holy Ghost.
*Bp. Thomas Ken. ab.*

## BRIGHTEST AND BEST.

Brightest and best of the sons of the morning,
  Dawn on our darkness, and lend us Thine aid;
Star of the East, the horizon adorning,
  Guide where our infant Redeemer is laid.

Cold on His cradle the dew-drops are shining,
  Low lies His head with the beasts of the stall;
Angels adore Him, in slumber reclining,
  Maker and Monarch and Saviour of all!

Say, shall we yield Him, in costly devotion,
  Odors of Edom, and offerings divine,
Gems of the mountain and pearls of the ocean,
  Myrrh from the forest or gold from the mine?

Vainly we offer each ample oblation,
  Vainly with gifts would His favor secure;
Richer by far is the heart's adoration,
  Dearer to God are the prayers of the poor.

Brightest and best of the sons of the morning,
  Dawn on our darkness, and lend us Thine aid;
Star of the East, the horizon adorning,
  Guide where our infant Redeemer is laid.

*Bp. Reginald Heber.*

---

### O COME, ALL YE FAITHFUL.

O come, all ye faithful, triumphantly sing,
Come see in the manger the angels' dread King;
To Bethlehem hasten, with joyful accord;
O hasten, O hasten, to worship the Lord.

True Son of the Father, He comes from the skies;
The womb of the Virgin He doth not despise;
To Bethlehem hasten, with joyful accord;
O hasten, O hasten, to worship the Lord.

O hark to the angels, all singing in heaven,
"To God in the highest, all glory be given."
To Bethlehem hasten, with joyful accord,
O hasten, O hasten, to worship the Lord.

To Thee, then, O Jesus, this day of Thy birth,
Be glory and honor through heaven and earth;
True Godhead Incarnate, Omnipotent Word:
O hasten, O hasten, to worship the Lord.

*Unknown Author, of uncertain date.*
*Tr. by Rev. Edward Caswall.*

---

## MY HEART THIS NIGHT REJOICES.

All my heart this night rejoices,
  As I hear,
  Far and near,
 Sweetest angel voices:
"Christ is born," their choirs are singing,
  Till the air
  Everywhere
 Now with joy is ringing.

## My Heart this Night rejoices.

Hark! a voice from yonder manger,
  Soft and sweet,
  Doth entreat:
 "Flee from woe and danger;
Brethren, come: from all that grieves you
  You are freed;
  All you need
 I will surely give you."

Come, then, let us hasten yonder;
  Here let all,
  Great and small,
 Kneel in awe and wonder;
Love Him who with love is yearning;
  Hail the Star
  That from far
 Bright with hope is burning!

Ye who pine in weary sadness,
  Weep no more,
  For the door
 Now is found of gladness.
Cling to Him, for He will guide you
  Where no cross,
  Pain or loss,
 Can again betide you.

Hither come, ye heavy-hearted,
  Who for sin,
  Deep within,
 Long and sore have smarted:

## My Heart this Night rejoices.

For the poisoned wounds you're feeling
      Help is near;
      One is here
Mighty for their healing.
Hither come, ye poor and wretched,
      Know His will
      Is to fill
Every hand outstretchèd;
Here are riches without measure,
      Here forget
      All regret,
Fill your hearts with treasure.

Blessed Saviour, let me find Thee!
      Keep Thou me
      Close to Thee,
Cast me not behind Thee!
Life of life, my heart Thou stillest,
      Calm I rest
      On Thy breast,
All this void Thou fillest.
Heedfully my Lord I'll cherish,
      Live to Thee,
      And with Thee
Dying shall not perish;
But shall dwell with Thee forever,
      Far on high,
      In the joy
That can alter never.

*Rev. Paul Gerhardt.*
*Tr. by Miss Catherine Winkworth ab.*

## HARK! WHAT MEAN THOSE VOICES?

Hark! what mean those holy voices
    Sweetly warbling in the skies?
Sure the angelic host rejoices,
    Loudest hallelujahs rise.
        Hallelujah!

Listen to the wondrous story,
    Which they chant in hymns of joy:
"Glory in the highest, glory,
    Glory be to God most high!
        Hallelujah!

"Peace on earth, good will from heaven,
    Reaching far as man is found;
Souls redeemed, and sins forgiven,
    Loud our golden harps shall sound.
        Hallelujah!

"Christ is born, the great Anointed!
    Heaven and earth His glory sing!
Glad receive whom God appointed
    For your Prophet, Priest and King.
        Hallelujah!

"Hasten, mortals, to adore Him,
    Learn His name and taste His joy,
Till in heaven you sing before Him,
    Glory be to God most high!
        Hallelujah!"

Let us learn the wondrous story
   Of our great Redeemer's birth,
Spread the brightness of His glory,
   Till it cover all the earth.
      Hallelujah!

*Rev. John Cawood.*

## OF THE FATHER'S LOVE BEGOTTEN.

Of the Father's love begotten,
   Ere the worlds began to be,
He is Alpha and Omega,
   He the source, the ending He,
Of the things that are, that have been,
   And the future years shall see,
     Evermore and evermore!

He is here, whom seers in old time
   Chanted of, while ages ran;
Whom the voices of the Prophets
   Promised since the world began:
Then foretold, now manifested,
   To receive the praise of man,
     Evermore and evermore!

Oh that ever-blessed birthday,
   When the Virgin, full of grace,
Of the Holy Ghost incarnate
   Bare the Saviour of our race;

### Of the Father's Love begotten.

And that Child, the world's Redeemer,
   First displayed His Sacred Face,
     Evermore and evermore!

Praise Him, O ye heavens of heavens!
   Praise Him, angels in the height!
Every power and every virtue
   Sing the praise of God aright!
Let no tongue of man be silent,
   Let each heart and voice unite,
     Evermore and evermore!

Thee let age, and Thee let manhood,
   Thee let choirs of infants sing;
Thee the matrons and the virgins,
   And the children answering:
Let their modest song re-echo,
   And their heart its praises bring,
     Evermore and evermore!

Laud and honor to the Father!
   Laud and honor to the Son!
Laud and honor to the Spirit!
   Ever Three and ever One:
Consubstantial, co-eternal,
   While unending ages run,
     Evermore and evermore!
     *Tr. from "Clemens Auretius Prudentius."*

## IT CAME UPON THE MIDNIGHT CLEAR.

It came upon the midnight clear,
    That glorious song of old,
From angels bending near the earth
    To touch their harps of gold:
"Peace to the earth, good-will to men
    From heaven's all-gracious King!"
The world in solemn stillness lay
    To hear the angels sing.

Still through the cloven skies they come,
    With peaceful wings unfurled;
And still their heavenly music floats
    O'er all the weary world:
Above its sad and lowly plains
    They bend on heavenly wing,
And ever o'er its Babel sounds
    The blessed angels sing.

Yet with the woes of sin and strife
    The world has suffered long;
Beneath the angel-strain have rolled
    Two thousand years of wrong;
And men, at war with men, hear not
    The love-song which they bring:
Oh! hush the noise, ye men of strife
    And hear the angels sing!

And ye, beneath life's cr
    Whose forms are b;

**48** *At the Cross her Station keeping.*

Who toil along the climbing way
  With painful steps and slow,—
Look now! for glad and golden hours
  Come swiftly on the wing:
Oh! rest beside the weary road,
  And hear the angels sing!

For lo! the days are hastening on,
  By prophet-bards foretold,
When with the ever-circling years
  Comes round the age of gold;
When Peace shall over all the earth
  Its ancient splendors fling,
And the whole world send back the song
  Which now the angels sing.
              *Rev. Edmund Hamilton Sears.*

———•◊•———

## AT THE CROSS HER STATION KEEPING.

At the cross her station keeping,
Stood the mournful Mother weeping,
  Where He hung, her Son and Lord;
For her soul, of joy bereavèd,
Bowed with anguish, deeply grievèd,
  Felt the sharp and piercing sword.

      *Tr. fro-* nd sore distressèd
              t Mother blessèd
            "en One;

## At the Cross her Station keeping.

Deep the woe of her affliction
When she saw the Crucifixion
  Of her ever-glorious Son.

Who, on Christ's dear Mother gazing,
Pierced by anguish so amazing,
  Born of woman, would not weep?
Who, on Christ's dear Mother thinking,
Such a cup of sorrow drinking,
  Would not share her sorrows deep?

For His people's sins chastisèd
She beheld her Son despisèd,
  Scourged, and crowned with thorns entwined;
Saw Him then from judgment taken,
And in death by all forsaken,
  Till His Spirit He resigned.

. . . . .

Jesu, may such deep devotion
Stir in me the same emotion,
  Fount of love, Redeemer kind!
That my heart, fresh ardor gaining,
And a purer love attaining,
  May with Thee acceptance find.

*From the Latin of Jacopône.* ab.

## ALAS, AND DID MY SAVIOUR BLEED?

Alas, and did my Saviour bleed?
   And did my Sovereign die?
Would He devote that sacred head
   For such a worm as I?

Was it for crimes that I had done
   He groaned upon the tree?
Amazing pity! grace unknown!
   And love beyond degree!

Well might the sun in darkness hide,
   And shut his glories in,
When God, the mighty Maker, died
   For man the creature's sin.

Thus might I hide my blushing face,
   While His dear cross appears:
Dissolve, my heart, in thankfulness,
   And melt, mine eyes, to tears.

But drops of grief can ne'er repay
   The debt of love I owe:
Here, Lord, I give myself away;
   'Tis all that I can do.

*Rev. Isaac Watts. ab.*

## WHEN I SURVEY THE WONDROUS CROSS.

When I survey the wondrous cross
   On which the Prince of glory died,
My richest gain I count but loss,
   And pour contempt on all my pride.

Forbid it, Lord, that I should boast,
   Save in the death of Christ, my God!
All the vain things that charm me most,
   I sacrifice them to His blood.

See, from His head, His hands, His feet,
   Sorrow and love flow mingled down!
Did e'er such love and sorrow meet?
   Or thorns compose so rich a crown?

His dying crimson, like a robe,
   Spreads o'er His body on the tree;
Then am I dead to all the globe,
   And all the globe is dead to me.

Were the whole realm of nature mine,
   That were a present far too small;
Love so amazing, so Divine,
   Demands my soul, my life, my all.
                *Rev. Isaac Watts.*

## O SACRED HEAD! NOW WOUNDED.

O sacred Head! now wounded,
   With grief and shame weighed down,
Now scornfully surrounded
   With thorns, Thy only crown;
O sacred Head! what glory,
   What bliss, till now was Thine!
Yet, though despised and gory,
   I joy to call Thee mine.

O noblest brow, and dearest!
   In other days the world
All feared when Thou appearedst:
   What shame on Thee is hurled!
How art Thou pale with anguish,
   With sore abuse and scorn;
How does that visage languish,
   Which once was bright as morn!

The blushes late residing
   Upon that holy cheek,
The roses once abiding
   Upon those lips so meek,
Alas! they have departed;
   Wan Death has rifled all!
For weak and broken-hearted,
   I see Thy body fall.

What Thou, my Lord, hast suffered,
   Was all for sinners' gain:

## *O sacred Head! now wounded.*

Mine, mine, was the transgression,
   But Thine the deadly pain.
Lo! here I fall, my Saviour:
   'Tis I deserve Thy place;
Look on me with Thy favor,
   Vouchsafe to me Thy grace.

Receive me, my Redeemer:
   My Shepherd, make me Thine,
Of every good the fountain,
   Thou art the spring of mine.
Thy lips with love distilling,
   And milk of truth sincere,
With heaven's bliss are filling
   That soul that trembles here.

Beside Thee, Lord, I've taken
   My place—forbid me not!
Hence will I ne'er be shaken,
   Though Thou to death be brought,
If pain's last paleness hold Thee,
   In agony opprest,
Then, then, will I enfold Thee
   Within this arm and breast!

The joy can ne'er be spoken,
   Above all joys beside,
When in Thy body broken
   I thus with safety hide.
My Lord of life, desiring
   Thy glory now to see,

Beside the cross expiring,
  I'd breathe my soul to Thee.

What language shall I borrow
  To thank Thee, dearest Friend,
For this, Thy dying sorrow,
  Thy pity without end!
O make me Thine forever;
  And should I fainting be,
Lord, let me never, never
  Outlive my love to Thee.

And when I am departing,
  O part not Thou from me!
When mortal pangs are darting,
  Come, Lord, and set me free!
And when my heart must languish
  Amidst the final throe,
Release me from mine anguish
  By Thine own pain and woe!

Be near me when I'm dying,
  Oh! show Thy cross to me;
And for my succor flying,
  Come, Lord, and set me free!
These eyes new faith receiving
  From Jesus shall not move;
For he, who dies believing,
  Dies safely through Thy love.

*Rev. Paul Gerhardt.*
*Tr. by Rev. James W. Alexander.*

## CHRIST, THE LIFE OF ALL.

Christ, the Life of all the living,
   Christ, the Death of death, our foe,
Who Thyself for me once giving
   To the darkest depths of woe,
   Patiently didst yield Thy breath
   But to save my soul from death;
   Thousand, thousand thanks shall be,
   Blessed Jesus, unto Thee.

Thou, ah, Thou, hast taken on Thee
   Bitter strokes, a cruel rod;
Pain and scorn were heaped upon Thee
   O Thou sinless Son of God!
   Only Thus for me to win
   Rescue from the bonds of sin;
   Thousand, thousand thanks shall be,
   Blessed Jesus, unto Thee.

Thou didst bear the smiting only
   That it might not fall on me;
Stoodest falsely charged and lonely,
   That I might be safe and free;
   Comfortless, that I might know
   Comfort from Thy boundless woe;
   Thousand, thousand thanks shall be,
   Blessed Jesus, unto Thee.

Then for all that wrought our pardon,
   For Thy sorrows deep and sore,

For Thine anguish in the garden,
  I will thank Thee evermore;
Thank Thee with my latest breath
For Thy sad and cruel death;
For that last and bitter cry,
  Praise Thee evermore on high.
*From German of Ernst Christoph Homburg.*

---

## NOW, MY SOUL, THY VOICE UPRAISING.

Now, my soul, thy voice upraising,
  Tell in sweet and mournful strain,
How the Crucified, enduring
  Grief, and wounds, and dying pain,
Freely of His love was offered,
  Sinless was for sinners slain.

Scourged with unrelenting fury
  For the sins which we deplore,
By His livid stripes He heals us,
  Raising us to fall no more:
All our bruises gently soothing,
  Binding up the bleeding sore.

See, His hands and feet are fastened;
  So He makes His people free:
Not a wound whence blood is flowing
  But a fount of grace shall be;
Yea the very nails which nail Him
  Nail us also to the tree.

Through His heart the spear is piercing,
  Though His foes have seen Him die;
Blood and water thence are streaming
  In a tide of mystery,
Water from our guilt to cleanse us,
  Blood to win us crowns on high.

Jesus, may those precious fountains
  Drink to thirsting souls afford;
Let them be our cup and healing,
  And at length our full reward;
So a ransomed world shall ever
  Praise Thee, its redeeming Lord.

*Santolius Maglorianus.*
*Tr. by Rev. Sir Henry Williams Baker.*

———◆———

## THE ROYAL BANNERS FORWARD GO

The Royal Banners forward go,
The Cross shines forth in mystic glow;
Where He in flesh, our flesh Who made,
Our sentence bore, our ransom paid.

There, whilst He hung, His sacred side
By soldier's spear was opened wide,
To cleanse us in the precious flood
Of water mingled with His blood.

Fulfilled is all that David told
In true prophetic song of old,

## The Royal Banners forward go.

How God the nation's King should be,
For God is reigning from the Tree.

O Tree of Glory, Tree most fair!
Ordained those Holy Limbs to bear;
How bright in purple robe it stood,
The purple of a Saviour's blood!

Upon its arms, so widely flung,
The weight of this world's ransom hung:
The ransom He alone could pay,
Despoiling Satan of his prey.

With fragrance dropping from each bough
Sweeter than sweetest nectar Thou;
Decked with the fruit of peace and praise,
And glorious with triumphal lays.

Hail, Altar! hail, O Victim! Thee
Decks now Thy Passion's victory;
Where life for sinners death endured,
And life, by death, for man procured.

To Thee, Eternal Three in One,
Let homage meet by all be done:
As by the Cross Thou dost restore,
So rule and guide us evermore.

*Venantius Fortunatus.*
*Tr. by Rev. John Mason Neale*

## THERE IS A FOUNTAIN.

There is a fountain filled with blood
   Drawn from Immanuel's veins,
And sinners plunged beneath that flood
   Lose all their guilty stains.

The dying thief rejoiced to see
   That fountain in his day;
And there have I, as vile as he,
   Washed all my sins away.

Dear dying Lamb, Thy precious blood
   Shall never lose its power,
Till all the ransomed church of God
   Be saved, to sin no more.

E'er since, by faith, I saw the stream
   Thy flowing wounds supply,
Redeeming love has been my theme,
   And shall be till I die.

Then, in a nobler, sweeter song,
   I'll sing Thy power to save,
When this poor lisping, stammering tongue
   Lies silent in the grave.

Lord, I believe Thou hast prepared
   (Unworthy though I be)
For me a blood-bought, free reward,
   A golden harp for me!

'Tis strung and tuned for endless years,
  And formed by power Divine,
To sound in God the Father's ears
  No other name but Thine.
                    *William Cowper*

---

### HARK! THE VOICE OF LOVE.

Hark! the voice of love and mercy
  Sounds aloud from Calvary;
See! it rends the rocks asunder,
  Shakes the earth, and veils the sky:
    "It is finished!"
  Hear the dying Saviour cry.

"It is finished!" O what pleasure
  Do these charming words afford!
Heavenly blessings, without measure,
  Flow to us from Christ, the Lord:
    "It is finished!"
  Saints, the dying words record.

Finished all the types and shadows
  Of the ceremonial law;
Finished all that God had promised,
  Death and hell no more shall awe:
    "It is finished!"
  Saints, from hence your comfort draw.
                *Rev. Jonathan Evans*

## IN THE CROSS OF CHRIST I GLORY.

In the cross of Christ I glory,
    Towering o'er the wrecks of time;
All the light of sacred story
    Gathers round its head sublime.

When the woes of life o'ertake me,
    Hopes deceive, and fears annoy,
Never shall the cross forsake me;
    Lo! it glows with peace and joy.

When the sun of bliss is beaming
    Light and love upon my way,
From the cross the radiance streaming,
    Adds more lustre to the day.

Bane and blessing, pain and pleasure,
    By the cross are sanctified;
Peace is there that knows no measure;
    Joys that through all time abide.

In the cross of Christ I glory,
    Towering o'er the wrecks of time;
All the light of sacred story
    Gathers round its head sublime.

*Sir John Bowring*

## O JESUS, WE ADORE THEE.

O Jesus, we adore Thee,
  Upon the cross, our King:
We bow our hearts before Thee;
  Thy gracious Name we sing:
That Name hath brought salvation,
  That Name, in life our stay;
Our peace, our consolation
  When life shall fade away.

Yet doth the world disdain Thee,
  Still passing by Thy cross:
Lord, may our hearts retain Thee;
  All else we count but loss.
The grief Thy soul endured,
  Who can that grief declare?
Thy pains have thus assuréd
  That Thou Thy foes wilt spare.

Ah, Lord, our sins arraigned Thee,
  And nailed Thee to the tree:
Our pride, O Lord, disdained Thee;
  Yet deign our Hope to be.
O glorious King, we bless Thee,
  No longer pass Thee by;
O Jesus, we confess Thee
  Our Lord enthroned on high.

Thy wounds, Thy grief beholding,
  With Thee, O Lord, we grieve;

Thee in our hearts enfolding,
   Our hearts Thy wounds receive:
Lord, grant to us remission;
   Life through Thy death restore;
Yea, grant us the fruition
   Of life for evermore.
                 *Rev. Arthur Tozer Russel.*

## JESUS, THY BLOOD.

Jesus, Thy Blood and Righteousness
My beauty are, my glorious dress;
'Midst flaming worlds, in these arrayed,
With joy shall I lift up my head.

Bold shall I stand in Thy great day,
For who aught to my charge shall lay?
Fully absolved through these I am,
From sin and fear, from guilt and shame.

The holy, meek, unspotted Lamb,
Who from the Father's bosom came,
Who died for me, e'en me to atone,
Now for my Lord and God I own.

Lord, I believe Thy precious blood,
Which at the mercy-seat of God
Forever doth for sinners plead,
For me—e'en for my soul—was shed.

## Jesus, thy Blood.

Lord, I believe were sinners more
Than sands upon the ocean shore,
Thou hast for all a ransom paid,
For all a full atonement made.

When from the dust of death I rise
To claim my mansion in the skies,
E'en then, this shall be all my plea:
Jesus hath lived, hath died for me.

Thus Abraham, the Friend of God,
Thus all heaven's armies bought with blood,
Saviour of sinners, Thee proclaim;
Sinners of whom the chief I am.

Jesus, be endless praise to Thee,
Whose boundless mercy hath for me,
For me, and all Thy hands have made,
An everlasting ransom paid.

Ah! give to all Thy servants, Lord,
With power to speak Thy gracious word;
That all who to Thy wounds will flee,
May find eternal life in Thee.

Thou, God of power, Thou, God of love,
Let the whole world Thy mercy prove!
Now let Thy word o'er all prevail;
Now take the spoils of death and hell.

*Nikolaus Ludwig Zinzendorf. ab.*
*Tr. by Rev. John Wesley.*

## SWEET THE MOMENTS.

Sweet the moments, rich in blessing,
   Which before the cross I spend;
Life and health and peace possessing,
   From the sinner's dying Friend.
Here I'll sit, forever viewing
   Mercy's streams in streams of blood:
Precious drops, my soul bedewing,
   Plead and claim my peace with God.

Truly blessed is this station,
   Low before His cross to lie;
While I see Divine compassion
   Floating in His languid eye.
Here it is I find my heaven,
   While upon the Lamb I gaze;
Love I much? I've much forgiven,—
   I'm a miracle of grace.

Love and grief my heart dividing,
   With my tears His feet I'll bathe;
Constant still, in faith abiding,
   Life deriving from His death.
May I still enjoy this feeling,
   In all need to Jesus go;
Prove His wounds each day more healing,
   And Himself most deeply know!

*Rev. Walter Shirley.*

## THE MORNING PURPLES ALL THE SKY.

The morning purples all the sky,
    The air with praises rings;
Defeated hell stands sullen by,
    The world exulting sings:
Glory to God! our glad lips cry;
    All praise and worship be
On earth, in heaven, to God Most High,
    For Christ's great victory!

While He, the King all strong to save,
    Rends the dark doors away,
And through the breaches of the grave
    Strides forth into the day.
Glory to God! our glad lips cry;
    All praise and worship be
On earth, in heaven, to God Most High,
    For Christ's great victory!

Death's captive, in his gloomy prison
    Fast fettered He has lain;
But He has mastered death, is risen,
    And death wears now the chain.
Glory to God! our glad lips cry;
    All praise and worship be
On earth, in heaven, to God Most High,
    For Christ's great victory!

The shining angels cry, "Away
    With grief; no spices bring;

Not tears, but songs, this joyful day,
  Should greet the rising King!"
Glory to God! our glad lips cry;
  All praise and worship be
On earth, in heaven, to God Most High,
  For Christ's great victory!

That Thou our Paschal Lamb mayst be,
  And endless joy begin,
Jesus, Deliverer, set us free
  From the dread death of sin.
Glory to God! our glad lips cry;
  All praise and worship be
On earth, in heaven, to God Most High,
  For Christ's great victory!

*Rev. Alexander R. Thompson.*

---

## HALLELUJAH! HALLELUJAH!

Hallelujah! Hallelujah!
Finished is the battle now:
The crown is on the Victor's brow!
    Hence with sadness!
    Sing with gladness,
        Hallelujah!

Hallelujah! Hallelujah!
After sharp death that Him befell,
Jesus Christ hath conquered hell.

*Hallelujah! Hallelujah!*

    Earth is singing,
    Heaven is ringing,
        Hallelujah!

Hallelujah! Hallelujah!
On the third morning He arose,
Bright with victory o'er His foes.
    Sing we lauding,
    And applauding,
        Hallelujah!

Hallelujah! Hallelujah!
He hath closed hell's brazen door,
And heaven is open evermore!
    Hence with sadness!
    Sing with gladness,
        Hallelujah!

Hallelujah! Hallelujah!
Lord, by Thy wounds we call on Thee,
So from ill death to set us free,
    That our living
    Be thanksgiving!
        Hallelujah!
        *Latin Hymn of Twelfth Century.*
        *Tr. by Rev. John Mason Neale.*

## TO HIM, WHO FOR OUR SINS.

To Him, who for our sins was slain,
To Him, for all His dying pain,
      Sing we Hallelujah!
To Him, the Lamb our sacrifice,
Who gave His soul our ransom-price,
      Sing we Hallelujah!

To Him, who died that we might die
To sin, and live with Him on high,
      Sing we Hallelujah!
To Him, who rose that we might rise
And reign with Him beyond the skies,
      Sing we Hallelujah!

To Him, who now for us doth plead
And helpeth us in all our need,
      Sing we Hallelujah!
To Him, who doth prepare on high
Our home in immortality,
      Sing we Hallelujah!

To Him be glory evermore;
Ye heavenly hosts, your Lord adore;
      Sing we Hallelujah!
To Father, Son, and Holy Ghost,
One God most great, our joy and boast,
      Sing we Hallelujah!
      *Rev. Arthur Tozer Russel.*

## 'TIS THE DAY OF RESURRECTION.

'Tis the day of Resurrection,
 Earth! tell it out abroad!
The Passover of gladness!
 The Passover of God!
From Death to life Eternal,—
 From this world to the sky,
Our Christ hath brought us over,
 With hymns of victory.

Our hearts be pure from evil,
 That we may see aright
The Lord in rays eternal
 Of resurrection light:
And, listening to His accents,
 May hear, so calm and plain,
His own *"All hail!"*—and hearing,
 May raise the victor strain!

Now let the heavens be joyful!
 Let earth her song begin!
Let the round world keep triumph,
 And all that is therein:
Invisible and visible
 Their notes let all things blend,—
For Christ the Lord hath risen,
 Our joy that hath no end.

*John of Damascus.*<br>Tr. by Rev. *John Mason Neale.*

## COME, YE FAITHFUL.

Come, ye faithful, raise the strain
   Of triumphant gladness!
God hath brought His Israel
   Into joy from sadness.
Loosed from Pharaoh's bitter yoke
   Jacob's sons and daughters;
Led them with unmoistened foot
   Through the Red Sea waters.

'Tis the spring of souls to-day:
   Christ hath burst His prison;
And from three days' sleep in death,
   As a sun, hath risen.
All the winter of our sins,
   Long and dark, is flying
From His light, to whom we give
   Laud and praise undying.

Now the queen of seasons, bright
   With the day of splendor,
With the royal Feast of feasts,
   Comes its joy to render:
Comes to glad Jerusalem,
   Who with true affection
Welcomes, in unwearied strains,
   Jesu's Resurrection.

Neither might the gates of death,
   Nor the tomb's dark portal,

Nor the watchers, nor the seal,
  Hold Thee as a mortal:
But to-day admidst the twelve
  Thou didst stand, bestowing
That Thy peace, which evermore
  Passeth human knowing.

*John of Damascus.*
*Tr. by Rev. John Mason Neale.*

---

**STILL THY SORROW, MAGDALENA.**

Still thy sorrow, Magdalena!
  Wipe the tear-drops from thine eyes;
Not at Simon's board Thou kneelest,
  Pouring thy repentant sighs:
All with thy glad heart rejoices;
All things sing with happy voices,
    Hallelujah!

Laugh with rapture, Magdalena!
  Be thy drooping forehead bright;
Banished now is every anguish,
  Breaks anew thy morning light:
Christ from death the world hath freed;
He is risen, is risen indeed:
    Hallelujah?

Joy! exult, O Magdalena!
  He hath burst the rocky prison;
Ended are the days of darkness;
  Conqueror hath He arisen.

Mourn no more the Christ departed;
Run to welcome Him, glad-hearted:
    Hallelujah!

Lift thine eyes, O Magdalena!
   See! thy living Master stands;
See His face, as ever, smiling;
   See those wounds upon His hands,
On His feet, His sacred side,—
Gems that deck the Glorified;
    Hallelujah!

Live, now live, O Magdalena!
   Shining is thy new-born day;
Let thy bosom pant with pleasure,
   Death's poor terror flee away;
Far from thee the tears of sadness,
Welcome love, and welcome gladness!
    Hallelujah!

*From the Latin.*<br>*Tr. by Rev. Edward A. Washburn.*

---

## SEE, THE CONQUEROR.

See, the Conqueror mounts in triumph,
   See the King in royal state,
Riding on the clouds His chariot
   To His heavenly palace-gate;

Hark, the choirs of angel-voices
    Joyful Hallelujahs sing!
And the portals high are lifted,
    To receive their heavenly King.

Who is this that comes in glory,
    With the trump of Jubilee?
Lord of battles, God of armies,
    He has gained the victory;
He who on the cross did suffer,
    He who from the grave arose,
He has vanquished sin and Satan,
    He by death hath spoiled His foes.

Now our heavenly Aaron enters,
    With His blood within the veil;
Joshua now is come to Canaan,
    And the kings before Him quail;
Now He plants the tribes of Israel
    In their promised resting-place;
Now our great Elijah offers
    Double portion of His grace.

Thou hast raised our human nature
    On the clouds to God's right hand;
There we sit in heavenly places,
    There with Thee in glory stand;
Jesus reigns, adored by angels;
    Man with God is on the throne;
Mighty Lord, in Thine Ascension
    We by faith behold our own.

*He is gone; beyond the Skies.*

Lift us up from earth to heaven,
   Give us wings of faith and love,
Gales of holy aspirations
   Wafting us to realms above;
That, with hearts and minds uplifted,
   We with Christ our Lord may dwell,
Where He sits enthroned in glory
   In the heavenly citadel.

So at last, when He appeareth,
   We from out our graves may spring,
With our youth renewed like eagles',
   Flocking round our heavenly King,
Caught up on the clouds of heaven,
   And may meet Him in the air,
Rise to realms where He is reigning,
   And may reign forever there.
        *Bp. Christopher Wordsworth.* ab.

## HE IS GONE; BEYOND THE SKIES.

He is gone; beyond the skies,
A cloud receives Him from our eyes,
Gone beyond the highest height
Of mortal gaze or angel's flight;
Through the veils of time and space,
Passed into the holiest place;
All the toil, the sorrow done,
All the battle fought and won.

## He is gone; beyond the Skies.

He is gone; and we return,
And our hearts within us burn;
Olivet no more shall greet,
With welcome shout His coming feet;
Never shall we track Him more
On Gennesareth's glistening shore;
Never in that look or voice
Shall Zion's walls again rejoice.

He is gone; and we remain
In this world of sin and pain,
In the void which He has left;
On this earth of Him bereft,
We have still His work to do,
We can still His path pursue;
Seek Him both in friend or foe,
In ourselves His image show.

He is gone; but we once more
Shall behold Him as before,
In the heaven of heavens the same
As on earth He went and came;
In the many mansions there,
Place for us He will prepare;
In that world, unseen, unknown,
He and we may yet be one.

He is gone, but not in vain;
Wait until He comes again;
He is risen, He is not here;
Far above this earthly sphere,

*Our Lord is risen.*

Evermore in heart and mind,
There our peace in Him we find;
To our own Eternal Friend
Thitherward let us ascend.
   *Rev. Arthur Penrhyn Stanley*

---

### OUR LORD IS RISEN.

Our Lord is risen from the dead:
 Our Jesus is gone up on high;
The powers of hell are captive led,
 Dragged to the portals of the sky.
There His triumphant chariot waits,
 And angels chant the solemn lay:
Lift up your heads, ye heavenly gates,
 Ye everlasting doors, give way!

Loose all your bars of massy light,
 And wide unfold the ethereal scene:
He claims these mansions as His right;
 Receive the King of glory in!
Who is the King of glory? who?
 The Lord who all our foes o'ercame,
The world, sin, death, and hell o'erthrew;
 And Jesus is the Conqueror's name.

Lo! His triumphant chariot waits,
 And angels chant the solemn lay:
Lift up your heads, ye heavenly gates;
 Ye everlasting doors, give way!

Who is the King of glory? who?
   The Lord, of glorious power possessed,
The King of saints and angels too;
   God over all, forever blest!

*Rev. Charles Wesley.*

---

### ALL HAIL THE POWER.

All hail the power of Jesus' name!
   Let angels prostrate fall;
Bring forth the royal diadem,
   To crown Him Lord of all!

Let high-born seraphs tune the lyre,
   And, as they tune it, fall
Before His face who tunes their choir,
   And crown Him Lord of all!

Crown Him, ye morning-stars of light!
   Who fixed this floating ball;
Now hail the strength of Israel's might,
   And crown Him Lord of all!

Crown Him, ye martyrs of our God,
   Who from His altar call;
Extol the Stem of Jesse's rod,
   And crown Him Lord of all!

Ye seed of Israel's chosen race,
   Ye ransomed of the fall,
Hail Him who saves you by His grace,
   And crown Him Lord of all!

Hail Him, ye heirs of David's line,—
    Whom David Lord did call,—
The God incarnate, Man Divine,
    And crown Him Lord of all!

Sinners, whose love can ne'er forget
    The wormwood and the gall,
Go spread your trophies at His feet,
    And crown Him Lord of all!

Let every tribe and every tongue
    On this terrestrial ball,
To Him all majesty ascribe,
    And crown Him Lord of all!

*Rev. Edward Perronet.*

## THE HEAD THAT ONCE WAS CROWNED.

The Head that once was crowned with thorns
    Is crowned with glory now;
A royal diadem adorns
    The mighty Victor's brow.

The highest place that heaven affords
    Is His, is His by right,—
" The King of kings, and Lord of lords,"
    And heaven's eternal Light!

The joy of all who dwell above,
    The joy of all below,
To whom He manifests His love,
    And grants His name to know.

To them, the cross, with all its shame,
   With all its grace, is given;
Their name an everlasting name,
   Their joy the joy of heaven.

They suffer with their Lord below,
   They reign with Him above;
Their profit and their joy to know
   The mystery of His love.

The cross He bore is life and health,
   Though shame and death to Him;
His people's hope, His people's health,
   Their everlasting theme.
Rev. Thomas Kelly.

## SON OF GOD, TO THEE I CRY.

Son of God, to Thee I cry:
By the holy mystery
Of Thy dwelling here on earth;
By Thy pure and holy birth,
Lord, Thy presence let me see,
Manifest Thyself to me.

Lamb of God, to Thee I cry:
By Thy bitter agony,
By Thy pangs to us unknown,
By Thy Spirit's parting groan,
Lord, Thy presence let me see,
Manifest Thyself to me.

Prince of Life, to Thee I cry:
By Thy glorious majesty,
By Thy triumph o'er the grave,
Meek to suffer, strong to save,
Lord, Thy presence let me see,
Manifest Thyself to me.

Lord of glory, God most High,
Man exalted to the sky,
With Thy love my bosom fill,
Prompt me to perform Thy will;
Then Thy glory I shall see,
Thou wilt bring me home to Thee.
Bp. Richard Mant.

## I KNOW THAT MY REDEEMER LIVES.

I know that my Redeemer lives,
   And ever prays for me;
A token of His love He gives,
   A pledge of liberty.

I find Him lifting up my head,
   He brings salvation near;
His presence makes me free indeed,
   And He will soon appear.

Far spent is the Egyptian night
   Of fear, and pain, and grief;
And lo, I see the morning light
   That brings assured relief.

Jesus, I hang upon Thy word;
   I steadfastly believe
Thou wilt return, and claim me, Lord,
   And to Thyself receive.

When God is mine, and I am His,
   Of paradise possessed,
I taste unutterable bliss,
   And everlasting rest.

Rev. Charles Wesley.

## WE WERE NOT WITH THE FAITHFUL.

We were not with the faithful few
   Who stood Thy bitter cross around,
Nor heard Thy prayer for those that slew,
   Nor felt that earthquake rock the ground;
We saw no spear-wound pierce Thy side:
Yet we believe that Thou hast died.

No angel's message met our ear
   On that first glorious Easter day,—
"The Lord is risen. He is not here:
   Come, see the place where Jesus lay!"
But we believe that Thou didst quell
The banded powers of death and hell.

We saw Thee not return on high;
   And now, our longing sight to bless,
No ray of glory from the sky

Shines down upon our wilderness:
Yet we believe that Thou art there,
And seek Thee, Lord, in praise and prayer.
*From the Canterbury Hymnal.*

---

**JESUS, I MY CROSS HAVE TAKEN.**

Jesus, I my cross have taken,
   All to leave and follow Thee;
Destitute, despised, forsaken,
   Thou from hence my all shalt be.
Perish every fond ambition,
   All I've sought or hoped or known;
Yet how rich is my condition!
   God and heaven are still my own.

Let the world despise and leave me;
   They have left my Saviour too;
Human hearts and looks deceive me:
   Thou art not like them, untrue.
And while Thou shalt smile upon me,
   God of wisdom, love, and might!
Foes may hate, and friends may shun me
   Show Thy face and all is bright.

Go, then, earthly fame and treasure;
   Come, disaster, scorn and pain:
In Thy service pain is pleasure;
   With Thy favor, loss is gain.

## 84 *Jesus, I my Cross have taken.*

I have called Thee Abba, Father,
    I have stayed my heart on Thee:
Storms may howl, and clouds may gather
    All must work for good to me.

Man may trouble and distress me,
    'Twill but drive me to Thy breast;
Life with trials hard may press me,
    Heaven will bring me sweeter rest.
Oh, 'tis not in grief to harm me,
    While Thy love is left to me!
Oh, 'twere not in joy to charm me,
    Were that joy unmixed with Thee!

Take, my soul, thy full salvation!
    Rise o'er sin and fear and care;
Joy to find, in every station,
    Something still to do or bear.
Think what spirit dwells within thee,
    What a Father's smile is thine,
What a Saviour died to win thee;
    Child of heaven, should'st thou repine?

Haste, then, on from grace to glory,
    Armed by faith, and winged by prayer;
Heaven's eternal day's before thee,
    God's own hand shall guide thee there.
Soon shall close thy earthly mission,
    Swift shall pass thy pilgrim days;
Hope soon change to full fruition,
    Faith to sight, and prayer to praise.
        *Rev. Henry Francis Lyte.*

## JESU, NAME ALL NAMES ABOVE.

Jesu, name all names above,
   Jesu, best and dearest,
Jesu, Fount of perfect love,
   Holiest, tenderest, nearest!
Jesu, source of grace completest,
Jesu truest, Jesu sweetest,
   Jesu, Well of power divine,
   Make me, keep me, seal me Thine!

Jesu, open me the gate
   Which the sinner entered,
Who in his last dying state
   Wholly on Thee ventured.
Thou whose wounds are ever pleading,
And Thy passion interceding,
   From my misery let me rise
   To a home in Paradise!

Thou didst call the prodigal;
   Thou didst pardon Mary:
Thou whose words can never fall,
   Love can never vary,
Lord, amidst my lost condition
Give—for Thou canst give—contrition!
   Thou can'st pardon all mine ill:
   If Thou wilt, O say, "I will"!

Woe, that I have turned aside
   After fleshly pleasure!

## Jesu, Name all Names above.

Woe, that I have never tried
   For the heavenly treasure!
Treasure, safe in homes supernal;
Incorruptible, eternal!
    Treasure no less price hath won
    Than the Passion of the Son!

Jesu, crowned with thorns for me,
   Scourged for my transgression!
Witnessing, through agony,
   That Thy good confession;
Jesu, clad in purple raiment,
For my evils making payment;
    Let not all Thy woe and pain,
    Let not Calvary be in vain!

When I reach Death's bitter sea,
   And its waves roll higher,
Help the more forsaking me,
   As the storm draws nigher:
Jesu, leave me not to languish!
Helpless, hopeless, full of anguish!
    Tell me,—"Verily, I say,
    Thou shalt be with me to-day!"

*Theoctistus of the Studium.*
*Tr. by Rev. John Mason Neale.*

## JESU! THE VERY THOUGHT OF THEE

### I.

Jesu! the very thought of Thee
   With sweetness fills my breast;
But sweeter far Thy face to see,
   And in Thy presence rest.

Nor voice can sing, nor heart can frame,
   Nor can the memory find,
A sweeter sound than Thy blest name,
   O Saviour of mankind!

O Hope of every contrite heart,
   O Joy of all the meek!
To those who fall, how kind Thou art!
   How good to those who seek!

But what to those who find? Ah! this
   Nor tongue nor pen can show;
The love of Jesus, what it is,
   None but His loved ones know.

Jesu! our only joy be Thou,
   As Thou our prize shalt be;
Jesu! be Thou our glory now,
   And through eternity.

### II.

O Jesu! King most wonderful!
   Thou Conqueror renowned!
Thou Sweetness most ineffable,
   In whom all joys are found!

## 88 *Jesu! the very thought of Thee.*

When once Thou visitest the heart,
   Then truth begins to shine;
Then earthly vanities depart;
   Then kindles love divine.

O Jesu! Light of all below!
   Thou Fount of life and fire!
Surpassing all the joys we know,
   All that we can desire:

May every heart confess Thy name,
   And ever Thee adore;
And seeking Thee, itself inflame
   To seek Thee more and more.

Thee may our tongues forever bless;
   Thee may we love alone;
And ever in our lives express
   The image of Thine own.

### III.

O Jesu! Thou the beauty art
   Of angel worlds above;
Thy name is music to the heart,
   Enchanting it with love.

Celestial sweetness unalloyed!
   Who eat Thee hunger still;
Who drink of Thee still feel a void,
   Which nought but Thou can fill.

## Fairest Lord Jesus. 89

O my sweet Jesu! hear the sighs
   Which unto Thee I send;
To Thee mine inmost spirit cries,
   My being's hope and end!

Stay with us, Lord, and with Thy light
   Illume the soul's abyss;
Scatter the darkness of our night,
   And fill the world with bliss.

O Jesu! spotless virgin-flower!
   Our love and joy! to Thee
Be praise, beatitude, and power,
   Through all eternity.

*Bernard of Clairvaux.*
*Tr. by Rev. Edward Caswall.*

---

### FAIREST LORD JESUS.

Fairest Lord Jesus,
Ruler of nature!
Jesus, of God and of Mary the Son!—
Thee will I cherish,
Thee will I honor;
Thee, my delight and my glory and crown!

Fair are the meadows,
Fairer the woodlands,
Robed in the flowery vesture of spring:
Jesus is fairer,
Jesus is purer,
Making my sorrowful spirit to sing.

Fair is the moonshine,
Fairer the sunlight,
Than all the starry, celestial host:
Jesus shines brighter,
Jesus shines purer,
Than all the angels that heaven can boast.

*Anonymous. Twelfth Century.*

## AWAKE, MY SOUL.

Awake, my soul, in joyful lays,
And sing thy great Redeemer's praise;
He justly claims a song from me;
His loving-kindness, O how free!

He saw me ruined in the fall,
Yet loved me notwithstanding all;
He saved me from my lost estate;
His loving-kindness, O how great!

When I was Satan's easy prey,
And deep in debt and bondage lay,
He paid His life for my discharge;
His loving-kindness, O how large!

Through mighty hosts of cruel foes,
Where earth and hell my way oppose,
He safely leads my soul along;
His loving-kindness, O how strong!

When earthly friends forsake me quite,
And I have neither skill nor might,

He's sure my helper to appear;
His loving-kindness, O how near!

Often I feel my sinful heart
Prone from my Jesus to depart;
But though I have Him oft forgot,
His loving-kindness changes not!

When I shall pass death's gloomy vale,
And life and mortal powers must fail,
Oh! may my last expiring breath
His loving-kindness sing in death.

Then shall I mount and soar away
To the bright world of endless day;
And sing with rapture and surprise
His loving-kindness in the skies.

There with their golden harps I'll join,
And with their anthems mingle mine,
And loudly sound on every chord
The loving-kindness of my Lord.
*Rev. Samuel Medley.*

### JESU, MY LORD.

Jesu, my Lord, my God, my All,
Hear me, blest Saviour, when I call:
Hear me, and from Thy dwelling-place
Pour down the riches of Thy grace.
   Jesu, my Lord, I Thee adore;
   Oh make me love Thee more and more!

Jesu, too late I Thee have sought:
How can I love Thee as I ought;
And how extol Thy matchless fame,
The glorious beauty of Thy name?
 Jesu, my Lord, I Thee adore;
 Oh make me love Thee more and more!

Jesu, what didst Thou find in me,
That Thou hast dealt so lovingly?
How great the joy that Thou hast brought,
So far exceeding hope or thought:
 Jesu, my Lord, I Thee adore;
 Oh make me love Thee more and more!

Jesu, of Thee shall be my song:
To Thee my heart and soul belong;
All that I have or am is Thine,
And Thou, blest Saviour, Thou art mine.
 Jesu, my Lord, I Thee adore;
 Oh make me love Thee more and more!

*Rev. Henry Collins.*

---

## O LOVE DIVINE.

O love divine, how sweet Thou art!
When shall I find my willing heart
 All taken up by Thee?
I thirst and faint and die to prove
The greatness of redeeming love,
 The love of Christ to me!

Stronger His love than death or hell;
Its riches are unsearchable:
　　The first-born sons of light
Desire in vain its depth to see;
They cannot reach the mystery,
　　The length and breadth and height.

God only knows the love of God:
O that it now were shed abroad
　　In this poor stony heart!
For love I sigh, for love I pine:
This only portion, Lord, be mine,
　　Be mine this better part!

O that I could forever sit
With Mary at the Master's feet!
　　Be this my happy choice:
My only care, delight, and bliss,
My joy, my heaven on earth, be this,
　　To hear the Bridegroom's voice!

O that, with humbled Peter, I
Could weep, believe, and thrice reply,
　　My faithfulness to prove:
Thou know'st (for all to Thee is known),
Thou know'st, O Lord! and Thou alone,
　　Thou know'st that Thee I love.

O that I could, with favored John,
Recline my weary head upon
　　The dear Redeemer's breast!

From care and sin and sorrow free,
Give me, O Lord! to find in Thee
  My everlasting rest.

Thy only love do I require,
Nothing in earth beneath desire,
  Nothing in heaven above:
Let earth and heaven and all things go;
Give me Thy only love to know;
  Give me Thy only love.

*Rev. Charles Wesley.*

---

## JESUS, STILL LEAD ON.

Jesus, still lead on,
  Till our rest be won!
And, although the way be cheerless,
We will follow, calm and fearless:
  Guide us by Thy hand
  To our Fatherland!

If the way be drear,
  If the foe be near,
Let not faithless fears o'ertake us,
Let not faith and hope forsake us;
  For, through many a foe,
  To our home we go!

When we seek relief
  From a long-felt grief,

When temptations come alluring,
Make us patient and enduring:
    Show us that bright shore
    Where we weep no more!

Jesus, still lead on,
    Till our rest be won!
Heavenly Leader, still direct us,
Still support, console, protect us,
    Till we safely stand
    In our Fatherland!
        *Nikolaus Ludwig Zinzendorf.*
        *Tr. by Miss Jane Borthwick.*

---

## OH FOR A HEART!

Oh for a heart to praise my God!
    A heart from sin set free!
A heart that always feels Thy blood,
    So freely spilt for me!

A heart resigned, submissive, meek,
    My great Redeemer's throne!
Where only Christ is heard to speak,
    Where Jesus reigns alone:

A humble, lowly, contrite heart,
    Believing, true, and clean;
Which neither life nor death can part
    From Him that dwells within:

## *Jesus, I love thy Name.*

A heart in every thought renewed,
   And full of love divine;
Perfect and right, and pure and good,
   A copy, Lord, of Thine.

My heart, Thou knowest, can never rest
   Till Thou create my peace;
Till, of my Eden repossest,
   From every sin I cease.

Fruit of Thy gracious lips, on me
   Bestow that peace unknown;
The hidden manna, and the tree
   Of life, and the white stone.

Thy nature, gracious Lord, impart;
   Come quickly from above;
Write Thy new name upon my heart,
   Thy new, best name of Love.
                *Rev. Charles Wesley.*

---

## JESUS, I LOVE THY NAME.

Jesus, I love Thy charming name,
   'Tis music to mine ear;
Fain would I sound it out so loud
   That earth and heaven should hear.

Yes: Thou art precious to my soul,
   My transport and my trust;
Jewels to Thee are gaudy toys,
   And gold is sordid dust.

All my capacious powers can wish,
  In Thee doth richly meet;
Nor to mine eyes is light so dear
  Nor friendship half so sweet.

Thy grace still dwells upon my heart,
  And sheds its fragrance there;
The noblest balm of all its wounds,
  The cordial of its care.

I'll speak the honors of Thy name
  With my last laboring breath;
Then, speechless, clasp Thee in mine arms,
  The antidote of death.

*Rev. Philip Doddridge.*

---

JESUS, THY BOUNDLESS LOVE TO ME.

Jesus, Thy boundless love to me
  No thought can reach, no tongue declare
O knit my thankful heart to Thee
  And reign without a rival there!
Thine wholly, Thine alone, I am;
Be Thou alone my constant flame!

O grant that nothing in my soul
  May dwell but Thy pure love alone;
O may Thy love possess me whole,
  My joy, my treasure, and my crown:
Strange flames far from my heart remove;
May every act, word, thought, be love!

## Jesus, I love Thee.

O Love, how cheering is Thy ray!
  All pain before Thy presence flies:
Care, anguish, sorrow, melt away,
  Where'er Thy healing beams arise.
O Jesus, nothing may I see,
Nothing desire or seek, but Thee!

Still let Thy love point out my way!
  What wondrous things Thy love hath wrought!
Still lead me, lest I go astray;
  Direct my word, inspire my thought;
And if I fall, soon may I hear
Thy voice, and know that love is near.

In suffering, be Thy love my peace;
  In weakness, be Thy love my power;
And when the storms of life shall cease,
  Jesus, in that dark, final hour
Of death, be Thou my guide and friend.
That I may love Thee without end.

Rev. Paul Gerhardt.<br>Tr by Rev John Wesley.

---

### JESUS, I LOVE THEE

Jesus, I love Thee,—not because
  I hope for heaven thereby,
Nor yet because, if I love not,
  I must forever die.

## Jesus, I love Thee.

I love Thee, Saviour dear, and still
   I ever will love Thee,
Solely because my God Thou art,
   Who first hast lovèd me.

For me to lowest depths of woe
   Thou didst Thyself abase;
For me didst bear the cross and shame
   And manifold disgrace.

For me didst suffer pains unknown,
   Blood-sweat and agony,
Yea, death itself,—all, all for me,
   Who was Thine enemy.

Then why, O blessed Saviour mine!
   Should I not love thee well?
Not for the sake of winning heaven,
   Nor of escaping hell;

Not with the hope of gaining aught,
   Nor seeking a reward,—
But freely, fully, as Thyself
   Hast lovèd me, O Lord!

Even so I love Thee and will love,
   And in Thy praise will sing;
Solely because Thou art my God,
   And my eternal King.

*Francis Xavier.*
*Tr. by Rev. Edward Caswall.*

## O HOLY SAVIOUR, FRIEND UNSEEN!

O Holy Saviour, Friend unseen!
The faint, the weak, on Thee may lean;
Help me, throughout life's varying scene,
    By faith to cling to Thee.

Blest with communion so divine,
Take what Thou wilt, shall I repine,
When, as the branches to the vine,
    My soul may cling to Thee?

Far from her home, fatigued, opprest,
Here she has found a place of rest;
An exile still, yet not unblest,
    While she can cling to Thee.

Without a murmur I dismiss
My former dreams of earthly bliss:
My joy, my recompense, be this,—
    Each hour to cling to Thee.

What though the world deceitful prove,
And earthly friends and joys remove;
With patient, uncomplaining love,
    Still would I cling to Thee.

Oft when I seem to tread alone
Some barren waste, with thorns o'ergrown,
A voice of love, in gentlest tone,
    Whispers, "Still cling to Me."

Though faith and hope awhile be tried,
I ask not, need not, aught beside:
How safe, how calm, how satisfied,
    The souls that cling to Thee!

They fear not life's rough storms to brave,
Since Thou art near, and strong to save;
Nor shudder e'en at death's dark wave;
    Because they cling to Thee?

Blest is my lot, whate'er befall:
What can disturb me, who appall,
While, as my Strength, my Rock, my All,
    Saviour! I cling to Thee?
*Miss Charlotte Elliott.*

---

## LEAVE GOD TO ORDER ALL THY WAYS.

Leave God to order all thy ways,
    And hope in Him whate'er betide;
Thou'lt find Him in the evil days
    An all sufficient strength and guide.
Who trusts in God's unchanging love,
Builds on the rock that nought can move.

What can these anxious cares avail,
    These never-ceasing moans and sighs?
What can it help us to bewail
    Each painful moment as it flies?
Our cross and trials do but press
The heavier for our bitterness.

## Leave God to order all thy Ways.

Only your restless heart keep still,
   And wait in cheerful hope, content
To take whate'er His gracious will,
   His all-discerning love, hath sent;
Nor doubt our inmost wants are known
To Him who chose us for His own.

He knows when joyful hours are best,
   He sends them as He sees it meet;
When thou hast borne its fiery test,
   And now art freed from all deceit,
He comes to thee all unaware,
And makes Thee own His loving care.

Nor in the heat of pain and strife,
   Think God hath cast thee off unheard;
Nor that the man whose prosperous life
   Thou enviest, is of Him preferred;
Time passes and much change doth bring,
And sets a bound to everything.

All are alike before His face;
   'Tis easy to our God Most High
To make the rich man poor and base,
   To give the poor man wealth and joy.
True wonders still of Him are wrought,
Who setteth up and brings to nought.

Sing, pray, and swerve not from His ways,
   But do thine own part faithfully;
Trust His rich promises of grace,

So shall it be fulfilled in thee;
God never yet forsook at need
The soul that trusted Him indeed.
                      *George Neumark.*

## THOU ART MY HIDING PLACE.

Thou art my hiding place, O Lord,
   In Thee I put my trust,
Encouraged by Thy holy word,
   A feeble child of dust.
I have no argument beside,
   I urge no other plea;
And 'tis enough the Saviour died,
   My Saviour died for me.

When storms of fierce temptation beat,
   And furious foes assail,
My refuge is the mercy-seat,
   My hope within the veil.
From strife of tongues and bitter words
   My spirit flies to Thee:
Joy to my heart the thought affords,
   My Saviour died for me.

'Mid trials heavy to be borne,
   When mortal strength is vain,
A heart with grief and anguish tor
   A body rack'd with pain,—

Ah! what could give the sufferer rest,
    Bid every murmur flee,
But this, the witness in my breast
    That Jesus died for me?

And when Thine awful Voice commands
    This body to decay,
And life, in its last lingering sands,
    Is ebbing fast away,—
Then though it be in accents weak,
    And faint and tremblingly,
O give me strength in death to speak,
    My Saviour died for me.

*Rev. Thomas Raffles.*

## JESU, LOVER OF MY SOUL.

Jesu, lover of my soul,
    Let me to Thy bosom fly,
While the nearer waters roll,
    While the tempest still is high,
Hide me, O my Saviour! hide,
    Till the storm of life is past;
Safe into the haven guide,
    O receive my soul at last!

Other refuge have I none;
    Sing, hangs my helpless soul on Thee:
But oh! ah! leave me not alone;
    Trust Hi support and comfort me:

## Jesu, Lover of my Soul.

All my trust on Thee is stayed;
    All my help from Thee I bring;
Cover my defenceless head
    With the shadow of Thy wing.

Wilt Thou not regard my call?
    Wilt Thou not accept my prayer?
Lo! I sink, I faint, I fall;
    Lo! on Thee I cast my care.
Reach me out Thy gracious hand,
    While I of Thy strength receive;
Hoping against hope I stand,
    Dying, and behold I live!

Thou, O Christ! art all I want:
    More than all in Thee I find:
Raise the fallen, cheer the faint,
    Heal the sick, and lead the blind.
Just and holy is Thy name;
    I am all unrighteousness:
False and full of sin I am;
    Thou art full of truth and grace.

Plenteous grace with Thee is found,—
    Grace to cover all my sin:
Let the healing streams abound;
    Make and keep me pure within.
Thou of life the Fountain art;
    Freely let me take of Thee:
Spring Thou up within my heart
    Rise to all eternity.

                *Rev. Charles.*

## LOVE DIVINE.

Love Divine, all loves excelling,
    Joy of heaven, to earth come down,
Fix in us Thy humble dwelling,
    All Thy faithful mercies crown.
Jesus, Thou art all compassion,—
    Pure, unbounded love Thou art:
Visit us with Thy salvation,
    Enter every trembling heart.

Breathe, O breathe Thy loving Spirit
    Into every troubled breast!
Let us all in Thee inherit,
    Let us find that second rest.
Take away the love of sinning;
    Alpha and Omega be;
End of faith, as its beginning,
    Set our hearts at liberty.

Come, Almighty to deliver!
    Let us all Thy life receive;
Suddenly return, and never,
    Never more Thy temples leave.
Thee we would be always blessing,
    Serve Thee as Thy host above;
Pray, and praise Thee without ceasing,
    Sing, glory in Thy perfect love.

    But O, then, Thy new creation;
Trust Him, and spotless let us be;

Let us see Thy great salvation
  Perfectly secured by Thee,—
Changed from glory into glory,
  Till in heaven we take our place,—
Till we cast our crowns before Thee,
  Lost in wonder, love, and praise!
          *Rev. Charles Wesley.*

---

## JESUS' NAME SHALL EVER BE.

Jesus' name shall ever be
For my heart its Rosary.
I will tell it o'er and o'er,
Always dearer than before.

*Ave Mary* may not be
For my heart its Rosary;
Jesus, Saviour, all in all,—
Other name why should I call?

Morning hymns and evening lays,
Noontide prayer and midnight praise,
Heart and voice, and tune and time,
Jesus' name they all shall chime.

Ever new and fresh the strain;
Of all themes, the sweet refrain:
Time bring what it may along,
Jesus still the unchanging song.

Redolent with healing balm,
Pleasure's charm and trouble's calm;
All of heaven my hope and claim,
Grace on grace in Jesus' name.

In my soul each deepest chord
Ring it out, One Saviour Lord;
Jesus, the eternal hymn
Forth from saint and seraphim.

Breathe it, then, my every breath;
Linger on my last in death;
Jesus—Rest in Paradise;
Jesus—Glory in the skies!
*Rev. Wm. Augustus Muhlenberg.*

---

## IN THE SILENT MIDNIGHT.

In the silent midnight watches,
   List,—thy bosom door!
How it knocketh, knocketh, knocketh,
   Knocketh evermore!
Say not 'tis thy pulse is beating:
   'Tis thy heart of sin;
'Tis thy Saviour knocks, and crieth,
   Rise, and let Me in!

Death comes down, with reckless footstep,
   To the hall and hut:
Think you Death will stand a-knocking
   Where the door is shut?

Jesus waiteth, waiteth, waiteth;
   But thy door is fast!
Grieved, away thy Saviour goeth:
   Death breaks in at last.

Then 'tis thine to stand entreating
   Christ to let thee in;
At the gate of heaven beating,
   Wailing for thy sin.
Nay, alas! thou foolish virgin,
   Hast thou then forgot?
Jesus waited long to know thee,
   But He knows thee not!
        *Bp. Arthur Cleveland Coxe.*

---

## THE SAVIOUR! O, WHAT CHARMS.

The Saviour! O, what endless charms
   Dwell in that blissful sound!
Its influence every fear disarms,
   And spreads sweet comfort round.

Here pardon, life, and joys divine
   In rich effusion flow
For guilty rebels, lost in sin,
   And doomed to endless woe.

The almighty Former of the skies
   Stooped to our vile abode;
While angels viewed with wondering eyes,
   And hailed the incarnate God.

O the rich depths of love divine!
   Of bliss a boundless store!
Dear Saviour, let me call Thee mine;
   I cannot wish for more.

On Thee alone my hope relies;
   Beneath Thy cross I fall;
My Lord, my Life, my Sacrifice,
   My Saviour, and my All.
Miss Anne Steele. ab

---

### HOW SWEET THE NAME.

How sweet the name of Jesus sounds
   In a believer's ear!
It soothes his sorrows, heals his wounds,
   And drives away his fear.

It makes the wounded spirit whole,
   And calms the troubled breast;
'Tis manna to the hungry soul,
   And to the weary, rest.

Dear name! the rock on which I build,
   My shield and hiding-place;
My never-failing treasury, filled
   With boundless stores of grace.

By Thee, my prayers acceptance gain,
   Although with sin defiled;
Satan accuses me in vain,
   And I am owned a child.

## One, above all others.

Jesus! my Shepherd, Guardian, Friend
  My Prophet, Priest, and King;
My Lord, my Life, my Way, my End,
  Accept the praise I bring.

Weak is the effort of my heart,
  And cold my warmest thought;
But when I see Thee as Thou art,
  I'll praise Thee as I ought.

Till then I would Thy love proclaim,
  With every fleeting breath;
And may the music of Thy name
  Refresh my soul in death!
                    *Rev. John Newton.*

---

### ONE, ABOVE ALL OTHERS.

One there is, above all others,
  Well deserves the name of friend;
His is love beyond a brother's,
  Costly, free, and knows no end:
They who once His kindness prove,
Find it everlasting love.

Which of all our friends to save us,
  Could or would have shed their blood?
But our Jesus died to have us
  Reconciled in Him to God:
This was boundless love indeed,
Jesus is a friend in need.

Men, when raised to lofty stations,
 Often know their friends no more;
Slight and scorn their poor relations,
 Though they valued them before:
But our Saviour always owns
Those whom He redeemed with groans

When He lived on earth abasèd,
 Friend of sinners was His name;
Now, above all glory raisèd,
 He rejoices in the same:
Still He calls them brethren, friends,
And to all their wants attends.

Could we bear from one another
 What He daily bears from us?
Yet this glorious Friend and Brother
 Loves us, though we treat Him thus:
Though for good we render ill,
He accounts us brethren still.

Oh! for grace our hearts to soften;
 Teach us, Lord, at length to love.
We, alas! forget too often
 What a Friend we have above;
But, when home our souls are brought,
We will love Thee as we ought.

*Rev. John Newton.*

## I WAS A WANDERING SHEEP.

*Arte mirā, miro consilio,
Quærens ovem suam summus opilio,
Ut nos revocaret ab exitio.*—OLD HYMN

I was a wandering sheep,
  I did not love the fold;
I did not love my Shepherd's voice,
  I would not be controlled.
I was a wayward child,
  I did not love my home;
I did not love my Father's voice,
  I loved afar to roam.

The Shepherd sought His sheep,
  The Father sought His child;
They followed me o'er vale and hill,
  O'er deserts waste and wild.
They found me nigh to death,
  Famished and faint and lone;
They bound me with the bands of love,
  They saved the wandering one!

They spoke in tender love,
  They raised my drooping head;
They gently closed my bleeding wounds,
  My fainting soul they fed.
They washed my filth away,
  They made me clean and fair;
They brought me to my home in peace,—
  The long-sought wanderer!

Jesus my Shepherd is,
  'Twas He that loved my soul;
'Twas He that washed me in His blood,
  'Twas He that made me whole.
'Twas He that sought the lost,
  That found the wandering sheep;
'Twas He that brought me to the fold,
  'Tis He that still doth keep.

I was a wandering sheep,
  I would not be controlled;
But now I love my Shepherd's voice,—
  I love, I love the fold.
I was a wayward child,
  I once preferred to roam;
But now I love my Father's voice,—
  I love, I love His home!

*Rev. Horatius Bonar*

---

### REST OF THE WEARY.

Rest of the weary,
  Joy of the sad,
Hope of the dreary,
  Light of the glad;
Home of the stranger,
  Strength to the end,
Refuge from danger,
  Saviour and Friend!

Pillow where, lying,
  Love rests its head;

## I need Thee, precious Jesus.

Peace of the dying,
  Life of the dead;
Path of the lowly,
  Prize at the end,
Breath of the holy,
  Saviour and Friend!

When my feet stumble,
  I'll to Thee cry;
Crown of the humble,
  Cross of the high.
When my steps wander,
  Over me bend,
Truer and fonder,
  Saviour and Friend!

Ever confessing
  Thee, I will raise
Unto Thee blessing,
  Glory, and praise;
All my endeavor,
  World without end,
Thine to be ever,
Saviour and Friend!

*Rev. John Samuel Bewley Monsell*

---

## I NEED THEE, PRECIOUS JESUS.

I need Thee, precious Jesus,
  For I am full of sin;
My soul is dark and guilty,
  My heart is dead within:

## 116 *I need Thee, precious Jesus.*

I need the cleansing fountain
  Where I can always flee,
The blood of Christ most precious
  The sinner's perfect plea.

I need Thee, blessèd Jesus,
  For I am very poor;
A stranger and a pilgrim,
  I have no earthly store:
I need the love of Jesus
  To cheer me on my way,
To guide my doubting footsteps,
  To be my strength and stay.

I need Thee, blessèd Jesus;
  I need a friend like Thee,—
A friend to soothe and pity,
  A friend to care for me.
I need the Heart of Jesus
  To feel each anxious care,
To tell my every trial
  And all my sorrows share.

I need Thee, blessèd Jesus,
  And hope to see Thee soon,
Encircled with the rainbow,
  And seated on Thy throne!
There, with Thy blood-bought children
  My joy shall ever be,
To sing Thy praise, Lord Jesus,
  To gaze, my Lord, on Thee.

        *Rev. Frederick Whitefield.*

## WHEN THROUGH THE TORN SAIL.

When through the torn sail the wild tempest is streaming,
When o'er the dark wave the red lightning is gleaming,
Nor hope lends a ray, the poor seaman to cherish,
We fly to our Maker: "Help, Lord, or we perish!"

O Jesus! once tossed on the breast of the billow,
Aroused by the shriek of despair from Thy pillow,
Now seated in glory the mariner cherish,
Who cries in his danger: "Help, Lord, or we perish!"

And oh! when the whirlwind of passion is raging,
When hell in our heart his wild warfare is waging,
Arise in Thy strength, Thy redeemèd to cherish;
Rebuke the destroyer: "Help, Lord, or we perish!"

*Bp. Reginald Heber.*

## FROM EVERY STORMY WIND

From every stormy wind that blows,
From every swelling tide of woes,
There is a calm, a sure retreat:
'Tis found beneath the mercy-seat.

There is a place where Jesus sheds
"The oil of gladness" on our heads;
A place than all beside more sweet:
It is the blood-bought mercy-seat.

There is a spot where spirits blend,
Where friend holds fellowship with friend,
Though sundered far, by faith they meet
Around one common mercy-seat.

Ah! whither could we flee for aid,
When tempted, desolate, dismayed?
Or how the hosts of hell defeat,
Had suffering saints no mercy-seat?

There! there on eagle wings we soar.
And sin and sense molest no more;
And heaven comes down our souls to greet,
Where glory crowns the mercy-seat.

O may my hand forget her skill,
My tongue be silent, cold, and still,
This bounding heart forget to beat,
If I forget the mercy-seat!

*Rev. Hugh Stowell.*

## SAVIOUR! WHEN IN DUST.

Saviour! when, in dust, to Thee
Low we bow the adoring knee;
When, repentant, to the skies
Scarce we lift our weeping eyes:
Oh! by all the pains and woe
Suffered once for man below,
Bending from Thy Throne on high,
Hear our solemn Litany!

By Thy helpless infant years,
By Thy life of want and tears;
By Thy days of sore distress
In the savage wilderness;
By the dread mysterious hour
Of the insulting tempter's power:
Turn, oh! turn a favoring eye,
Hear our solemn Litany!

By the sacred griefs that wept
O'er the grave where Lazarus slept;
By the boding tears that flowed
Over Salem's loved abode;
By the anguished sigh that told
Treachery lurked within Thy fold:
From Thy seat above the sky,
Hear our solemn Litany!

By Thine hour of dire despair
By Thine agony of prayer;

By the cross, the nail, the thorn,
Piercing spear, and torturing scorn
By the gloom that veiled the skies
O'er the dreadful sacrifice:
Listen to our humble cry,
Hear our solemn Litany!

By Thy deep expiring groan;
By the sad sepulchral stone;
By the vault, whose dark abode
Held in vain the rising God:
O! from earth to heaven restored,
Mighty re-ascended Lord,
Listen, listen to the cry
Of our solemn Litany!

*Sir Robert Grant*

## WHEN GATHERING CLOUDS.

When gathering clouds around I view,
And days are dark, and friends are few
On Him I lean, who not in vain
Experienced every human pain:
He sees my wants, allays my fears,
And counts and treasures up my tears.

If aught should tempt my soul to stray
From heavenly wisdom's narrow way,
To fly the good I would pursue,
Or do the sin I would not do,

Still He, who felt temptation's power,
Shall guard me in that dangerous hour.

If wounded love my bosom swell,
Deceived by those I prized too well,
He shall His pitying aid bestow,
Who felt on earth severer woe;
At once betrayed, denied, or fled,
By those who shared His daily bread.

If vexing thoughts within me rise,
And sore dismayed my spirit dies,
Still He, who once vouchsafed to bear
The sickening anguish of despair,
Shall sweetly soothe, shall gently dry,
The throbbing heart, the streaming eye.

When sorrowing o'er some stone I bend,
Which covers all that was a friend,
And from his voice, his hand, his smile,
Divides me for a little while,
Thou, Saviour, seest the tears I shed,
For Thou didst weep o'er Lazarus dead.

And O! when I have safely past,
Through every conflict but the last,
Still, still unchanging, watch beside
My painful bed, for Thou hast died!
Then point to realms of endless day,
And wipe the latest tear away!
*Sir Robert Grant.*

## CLING TO THE CRUCIFIED.

*"Tecum volo vulnerari*
*Te libenter amplexari*
*In cruce desidero"*
　　　　OLD HYMN.

Cling to the Crucified!
His death is life to Thee,—
Life for eternity.
His pains thy pardon seal;
His stripes thy bruises heal,
His cross proclaims thy peace,
Bids every sorrow cease.
His blood is all to thee:
It purges thee from sin;
It sets thy spirit free;
It keeps thy conscience clean.
Cling to the crucified!

Cling to the Crucified!
His is a heart of love,
Full as the hearts above;
Its depths of sympathy
Are all awake for thee:
His countenance is light,
Even to the darkest night.
That love shall never change;
That light shall ne'er grow dim:
Charge thou thy faithless heart
To find its all in Him.
Cling to the Crucified!
　　　　*Rev. Horatius Bonar*

## I LAY MY SINS ON JESUS.

> "*Jesu, plena caritate*
> *Manus tuae perforatae*
> *Laxent mea crimina;*
> *Latus tuum lanceatum,*
> *Caput spinis coronatum,*
> *Haec sint medicamina.*"
>     OLD HYMN.

I lay my sins on Jesus,
 The spotless Lamb of God;
He bears them all, and frees us
 From the accursèd load.
I bring my guilt to Jesus,
 To wash my crimson stains
White in His blood most precious,
 Till not a stain remains.

I lay my wants on Jesus;
 All fulness dwells in Him:
He heals all my diseases,
 He doth my soul redeem.
I lay my griefs on Jesus,
 My burdens and my cares:
He from them all releases,
 He all my sorrows shares.

I rest my soul on Jesus,
 This weary soul of mine:
His right hand me embraces,
 I on His breast recline.

I love the name of Jesus,
    Immanuel, Christ, the Lord:
Like fragrance on the breezes,
    His name abroad is poured.

I long to be like Jesus,
    Meek, loving, lowly, mild:
I long to be like Jesus,
    The Father's holy Child.
I long to be with Jesus
    Amid the heavenly throng,
To sing with saints His praises,
    To learn the angel's song.

*Rev. Horatius Bonar*

---

## FIERCE WAS THE WILD BILLOW.

Fierce was the wild billow,
    Dark was the night;
Oars labored heavily,
    Foam glimmered white;
Trembled, the mariners;
    Peril was nigh;
Then said the God of God:
    "Peace! it is I!"

Ridge of the mountain-wave,
    Lower thy crest!
Wail of Euroclydon,
    Be thou at rest!

Sorrow can never be,
    Darkness must fly,
Where saith the Light of Light:
    "Peace! it is I!"

Jesu Deliverer!
    Come Thou to me!
Soothe Thou my voyaging
    Over life's sea!
Thou, when the storm of death
    Roars, sweeping by,
Whisper, O Truth of Truth!
    "Peace! it is I!"
*Anatolius, Patriarch of Constantinople.*
    *Tr. by Rev. John Mason Neale.*

## ART THOU WEARY?

Art thou weary, art thou languid,
    Are thou sore distrest?
"Come to me," saith One, "and coming
    Be at rest!"

Hath He marks to lead me to Him,
    If He be my Guide?
"In His feet and hands are wound-prints,
    And His side."

Is there diadem, as Monarch,
    That His brow adorns?
"Yea, a crown in very surety,
    But of thorns!"

If I find Him, if I follow,
  What His guerdon here?
"Many a sorrow, many a labor,
    Many a tear."

If I still hold closely to Him,
  What hath He at last?
"Sorrow vanquished, labor ended,
    Jordan past!"

If I ask Him to receive me,
  Will He say me nay?
"Not till earth, and not till heaven
    Pass away!"

Finding, following, keeping, struggling,
  Is He sure to bless?
"Angels, martyrs, prophets, virgins,
    Answer, Yes!"

*Stephen of St. Sabas.*
*Tr. by Rev. John Mason Neale.*

---

## JUST AS I AM.

Just as I am,—without one plea,
But that Thy blood was shed for me,
And that Thou bidst me come to Thee,
  O Lamb of God, I come!

Just as I am,—and waiting not
To rid my soul of one dark blot,
To Thee, whose blood can cleanse each spot,
  O Lamb of God, I come!

Just as I am,—though tossed about,
With many a conflict, many a doubt,
Fightings and fears within, without,
    O Lamb of God, I come!

Just as I am,—poor, wretched, blind;
Sight, riches, healing of the mind,
Yea, all I need in Thee to find,
    O Lamb of God, I come!

Just as I am,—Thou wilt receive,
Wilt welcome, pardon, cleanse, relieve
Because Thy promise I believe,
    O Lamb of God, I come!

Just as I am,—Thy love unknown
Has broken every barrier down;
Now to be Thine, yea, Thine alone,
    O Lamb of God, I come!

Just as I am,—of that free love
"The breadth, length, depth, and height"
    to prove,—
Here for a season, then above,—
    O Lamb of God, I come!

*Miss Charlotte Elliott.*

---

### OH FOR THE PEACE!

Oh for the peace which floweth as a river,
  Making life's desert places bloom and smile!

Oh for the faith to grasp heaven's bright
"forever,"
  Amid the shadows of earth's "little
while!"

"A little while," for patient vigil-keeping,
  To face the stern, to wrestle with the strong,
"A little while," to sow the seed with weeping,
  Then bind the sheaves, and sing the harvest-song.

"A little while," to wear the weeds of sadness,
  To pace with weary steps through miry ways;
Then to pour forth the fragrant oil of gladness,
  And clasp the girdle round the robe of praise.

"A little while," 'midst shadow and illusion,
  To strive, by faith, love's mysteries to spell;
Then read each dark enigma's bright solution
  Then hail sight's verdict, "He doth all things well."

"A little while," the earthen pitcher taking
  To wayside brooks, from far-off fountains fed;
Then the cool lip its thirst forever slaking
  Beside the fulness of the Fountain Head.

"A little while," to keep the oil from failing,
  "A little while," faith's flickering lamp to trim;
And then, the Bridegroom's coming footsteps hailing,
  To haste to meet Him with the bridal hymn.

And He, who is Himself the Gift and Giver,
  The future glory and the present smile,
With the bright promise of the glad "forever"
  Will light the shadows of the "little while."

*Mrs. Jane Crewdson.*

## ROCK OF AGES.

Rock of ages, cleft for me,
Let me hide myself in Thee!
Let the water and the blood,
From Thy riven side which flowed,
Be of sin the double cure,
Cleanse me from its guilt and power.

Not the labors of my hands,
Can fulfil Thy law's demands:
Could my zeal no respite know,
Could my tears forever flow,
All for sin could not atone,
Thou must save and Thou alone.

Nothing in my hand I bring,
Simply to Thy cross I cling;
Naked come to Thee for dress,
Helpless look to Thee for grace,
Foul I to the fountain fly,
Wash me, Saviour, or I die.

While I draw this fleeting breath;
When my eye-strings break in death;
When I soar through tracts unknown,
See Thee on Thy judgment throne,
Rock of ages, cleft for me,
Let me hide myself in Thee!

*Rev. Augustus Montague Toplady.*

## NOW I HAVE FOUND A FRIEND.

Now I have found a friend,
    Jesus is mine;
His love shall never end,
    Jesus is mine.
Though earthly joys decrease,
Though earthly friendships cease,
Now I have lasting peace,
    Jesus is mine;

## Now I have found a Friend.

Though I grow poor and old,
    Jesus is mine;
Though I grow faint and cold,
    Jesus is mine.
He shall my wants supply,
His precious blood is nigh,
Nought can my hope destroy,
    Jesus is mine.

When death is sent to me,
    Jesus is mine;
Welcome eternity,
    Jesus is mine.
He my redemption is,
Wisdom and righteousness,
Life, light, and holiness,
    Jesus is mine.

When earth shall pass away,
    Jesus is mine.
In the great judgment-day,
    Jesus is mine.
Oh! what a glorious thing,
Then to behold my King,—
On tuneful harp to sing,
    Jesus is mine.

Father, Thy name I bless,
    Jesus is mine;
Thine was the sovereign grace,
    Praise shall be Thine.

Spirit of holiness,
Sealing the Father's grace,
Thou mad'st my soul embrace
Jesus as mine.

*Henry Hope.*

---

## WITH TEARFUL EYES I LOOK.

With tearful eyes I look around;
  Life seems a dark and stormy sea.
Yet 'midst the gloom I hear a sound,
  A heavenly whisper, "Come to Me!"

It tells me of a place of rest,
  It tells me where my soul may flee:
Oh! to the weary, faint, opprest,
  How sweet the bidding, "Come to Me!"

When the poor heart with anguish learns
  That earthly props resigned must be,
And from each broken cistern turns,
  It hears the accents, "Come to Me!"

When against sin I strive in vain,
  And cannot from its yoke get free,
Sinking beneath the heavy chain,
  The words arrest me, "Come to Me!"

When nature shudders, loath to part
  From all I love, enjoy, and see;
When a faint chill steals o'er my heart,
  A sweet voice utters, "Come to Me!"

Come, for all else must fail and die,
    Earth is no resting place for thee;
Heavenward direct thy weeping eye;
    I am thy portion, "Come to Me!"

O Voice of mercy, Voice of love!
    In conflict, grief and agony,
Support me, cheer me, from above,
    And gently whisper, "Come to Me!"
Rev. Hugh White.

## I HEARD THE VOICE OF JESUS.

I heard the voice of Jesus say,
    "Come unto Me and rest;
Lay down, thou weary one, lay down
    Thy head upon My breast."
I came to Jesus as I was,
    Weary and worn and sad;
I found in Him a resting-place,
    And He has made me glad.

I heard the voice of Jesus say,
    "Behold! I freely give
The living water: thirsty one,
    Stoop down, and drink and live."
I came to Jesus, and I drank
    Of that life-giving stream;
My thirst was quenched, my soul revived,
    And now I live in Him.

I heard the voice of Jesus say,
  "I am this dark world's light;
Look unto Me, thy morn shall rise,
  And all thy day be bright."
I looked to Jesus, and I found
  In Him my Star, my Sun;
And in that light of life I'll walk
  Till travelling days are done.

*Rev. Horatius Bonar.*

---

## NEARER, MY GOD, TO THEE.

Nearer, my God, to Thee,
  Nearer to Thee:
E'en though it be a cross
  That raiseth me;
Still all my song shall be,
Nearer, my God, to Thee,
  Nearer to Thee.

Though like the wanderer,
  The sun gone down,
Darkness be over me,
  My rest a stone;
Yet in my dreams I'd be
Nearer, my God, to Thee,
  Nearer to Thee.

There let the way appear
  Steps unto heaven;

All that Thou send'st to me,
   In mercy given;
Angels to beckon me
Nearer, my God, to Thee,
   Nearer to Thee.

Then with my waking thoughts
   Bright with Thy praise,
Out of my stony griefs
   Bethel I'll raise:
So by my woes to be
Nearer, my God, to Thee,
   Nearer to Thee.

Or if on joyful wing
   Cleaving the sky,
Sun, moon, and stars forgot,
   Upward I fly,
Still all my song shall be,
Nearer, my God, to Thee,
   Nearer to Thee.
            *Sarah Flower Adams.*

---

## AMID LIFE'S WILD COMMOTION.

Amid life's wild commotion,
   Where nought the heart can cheer,
Who points beyond its ocean
   To heaven's brighter sphere?

Our feeble footsteps guiding,
   When from the path we stray,
Who leads to bliss abiding?
   Christ is our only WAY.

When doubts and fears distress us,
   And all around is gloom,
And shame and fear oppress us,
   Who can our souls illume?
Heaven's rays are round us gleaming,
   And making all things bright,
The sun of TRUTH is beaming
   In glory on our sight.

Who fills our hearts with gladness
   That none can take away?
Who shows us, 'midst our sadness,
   The distant realms of day?
'Mid fears of death assailing,
   Who stills the heart's wild strife?
'Tis Christ! our Friend unfailing,
   The WAY, the TRUTH, the LIFE.

*Carl Julius Asschenfeld.*
*Translator unknown.*

---

## WHEN ACROSS THE HEART.

When across the heart deep waves of sorrow
   Break, as on a dry and barren shore;
When hope glistens with no bright to-morrow,
   And the storm seems sweeping evermore;

When the cup of every earthly gladness
  Bears no taste of the life-giving stream;
And high hopes, as though to mock our sadness,
  Fade and die as in some fitful dream,—

Who shall hush the weary spirit's chiding?
  Who the aching void within shall fill?
Who shall whisper of a peace abiding,
  And each surging billow calmly still?

Only He whose wounded heart was broken
  With the bitter cross and thorny crown;
Whose dear love glad words of joy had spoken;
  Who His life for us laid meekly down.

Blessed Healer! all our burdens lighten;
  Give us peace, Thine own sweet peace, we pray;
Keep us near Thee till the morn shall brighten,
  And all mists and shadows flee away.

*From the Canterbury Hymnal.*

---

## TOSSED WITH ROUGH WINDS.

Tossed with rough winds, and faint with fear,
Above the tempest, soft and clear,
What still small accents greet mine ear?—
      'Tis I: be not afraid.

'Tis I who wash thy spirit white;
'Tis I who gave thy blind eyes sight;
'Tis I, thy Lord, thy Life, thy Light.
           'Tis I: be not afraid.

These raging winds, this surging sea,
Bear not a breath of wrath to thee;
That storm has all been spent on Me.
           'Tis I: be not afraid.

This bitter cup, I drank it first;
To thee it is no draft accurst;
The hand that gives it thee is pierced.
           'Tis I: be not afraid.

Mine eyes are watching by thy bed;
My arms are underneath thy head;
My blessing is around thee shed.
           'Tis I: be not afraid.

When on the other side thy feet
Shall rest,—'mid thousand welcomes sweet,
One well-known voice thy heart shall greet,—
           'Tis I: be not afraid.

From out the dazzling majesty,
Gently He'll lay His hand on thee,
Saying, "Belovèd, lovest thou Me?
'Twas not in vain I died for thee.
           'Tis I: be not afraid."

*Mrs. Andrew Paton Charles.*

## ABIDE WITH ME!

Abide with me! fast falls the eventide:
The darkness deepens; Lord, with me abide:
When other helpers fail, and comforts flee,
Help of the helpless, O abide with me!

Swift to its close ebbs out life's little day;
Earth's joys grow dim, its glories pass away;
Change and decay in all around I see;
O Thou who changest not, abide with me!

Not a brief glance I beg, a passing word;
But, as Thou dwell'st with Thy disciples, Lord,
Familiar, condescending, patient, free,—
Come, not to sojourn, but abide, with me!

Come not in terrors, as the King of kings;
But kind and good, with healing in Thy wings:
Tears for all woes, a heart for every plea;
Come, Friend of sinners, and thus 'bide with me!

Thou on my head, in early youth, didst smile;
And, though rebellious and perverse meanwhile,
Thou hast not left me, oft as I left Thee:
On to the close, O Lord, abide with me!

I need Thy presence every passing hour;
What but Thy grace can foil the Tempter's
  power?
Who like Thyself my guide and stay can
  be?
Through cloud and sunshine, Lord, abide
  with me!

I fear no foe, with Thee at hand to bless;
Ills have no weight, and tears no bitterness;
Where is Death's sting? where, Grave, thy
  victory?
I triumph still, if Thou abide with me!

Hold, then, Thy cross before my closing
  eyes!
Shine through the gloom, and point me to
  the skies!
Heaven's morning breaks, and earth's vain
  shadows flee;
In life, in death, O Lord, abide with me!
*Rev. Francis Henry Lyte.*

---

## I WOULD NOT LIVE ALWAY.

I would not live alway; I ask not to stay
Where storm after storm rises dark o'er the
  way;
A few lurid mornings, that dawn on us here,
Are enough for life's woes, full enough for
  its cheer.

## I would not live alway.

I would not live alway, thus fettered by sin,
Temptation without and corruption within;
E'en the rapture of pardon is mingled with fears,
And the cup of thanksgiving with penitent tears.

I would not live alway; no, welcome the tomb;
Since Jesus hath lain there, I dread not its gloom;
There sweet be my rest, till He bid me arise,
To hail Him in triumph descending the skies.

Who, who would live alway, away from his God;
Away from yon heaven, that blissful abode,
Where the rivers of pleasure flow o'er the bright plains,
And the noontide of glory eternally reigns?

Where the saints of all ages in harmony meet,
Their Saviour and brethren transported to greet;
While the anthems of rapture unceasingly roll,
And the smile of the Lord is the feast of the soul.

*Rev. William Augustus Muhlenberg.*

## TRUSTINGLY, TRUSTINGLY

Trustingly, trustingly,
   Jesus, to Thee
Come I: Lord, lovingly
   Come Thou to me!
Then shall I lovingly,
Then shall I joyfully,
   Walk here with Thee.

Peacefully, peacefully,
   Walk I with Thee;
Jesus, my Lord, Thou art
   All, all to me.
Peace Thou hast left us,
Thy peace hast given us;
   So let it be.

Whom but Thyself, O Lord!
   Have I above?
What have I left on earth?
   Only Thy love!
Come then, O Saviour! come:
Come then, O Spirit! come
   Heavenly Dove.

Happily, happily,
   Pass I along,
Eager to work for Thee,
   Earnest and strong.

Life is for service true,
Life is for battle too;
   Life is for song.

Hopefully, hopefully,
   Onward I go,
Cheerfully, cheerfully,
   Meet I the foe.
Crowns are awaiting us,
Glory prepared for us;
   Joys overflow.
*Rev. Horatius Bonar.*

---

## IF ONLY I HAVE THEE.

If only I have Thee,
If only mine Thou art,
   And to the grave
   Thy power to save
Upholds my faithful heart,—
Nought can then my soul annoy,
Lost in worship, love, and joy.

If only I have Thee,
I gladly all forsake.
   To follow on
   Where Thou hast gone,
My pilgrim staff I take;
Leaving other men to stray
In the bright, broad, crowded way.

## *If only I have Thee.*

If only I have Thee,
If only Thou art near,
   In sweet repose
   My eyes shall close,
Nor Death's dark shadow fear;
And Thy heart's flood through my breast,
Gently charm my soul to rest.

If only I have Thee,
Then all the world is mine;
   Like those who gaze
   Upon the rays
That from Thy glory shine,
Rapt in holy thought of Thee,
Earth can have no gloom for me.

Where only I have Thee,
There is my fatherland;
   For everywhere
   The gifts I share
From Thy wide-spreading hand;
And in all my human kind,
Long-lost brothers dear I find.

*From the German of Novalis.*
*Tr. by Rev. George Washington Bethune.*

## I KNOW IN WHOM I PUT MY TRUST.

I know in whom I put my trust,
   I know what standeth fast,
When all things here dissolve like dust,
   Or smoke before the blast:
I know what still endures, howe'er
   All else may quake and fall,
When lies the prudent men ensnare,
   And dreams the wise enthrall.

It is the Dayspring from on high,
   The adamantine Rock,
Whence never storm can make me fly,
   That fears no earthquake's shock;
My Jesus Christ, my sure Defence,
   My Saviour, and my Light,
That shines within, and scatters thence
   Dark phantoms of the night;

Who once was borne, betrayed, and slain,
   At evening to the grave;
Whom God awoke, who rose again,
   A Conqueror strong to save;
Who pardons all my sin, who sends
   His Spirit pure and mild;
Whose grace my every step befriends,
   Who ne'er forgets His child!

Therefore I know in whom I trust,
   I know what standeth fast,

When all things formed of earthly dust
  Are whirling in the blast:
The terrors of the final foe
  Can rob me not of this;
And this shall crown me once, I know,
  With never-fading bliss.

Ernst Moritz Ardut.<br>
Tr. by Miss Catharine Winkworth

---

## MY FAITH LOOKS UP TO THEE.

My faith looks up to Thee,
Thou Lamb of Calvary,
    Saviour divine!
Now hear me while I pray,
Take all my guilt away,
O let me from this day
    Be wholly Thine.

May Thy rich grace impart
Strength to my fainting heart,
    My zeal inspire;
As Thou hast died for me,
O may my love to Thee,
Pure, warm, and changeless be,—
    A living fire.

While life's dark maze I tread,
And griefs around me spread,
    Be Thou my guide;

Bid darkness turn to day,
Wipe sorrow's tears away,
Nor let me ever stray
    From Thee aside.

When ends life's transient dream,
When death's cold, sullen stream
    Shall o'er me roll;
Blest Saviour, then in love
Fear and distrust remove;
O, bear me safe above,—
    A ransomed soul.
*Rev. Ray Palmer.*

## HALLELUJAH! I BELIEVE!

Hallelujah! I believe!
  Now the giddy world stands fast,
Now my soul has found an anchor
  Till the night of storm is past.
All the gloomy mists are rising,
  And the clew is in my hand,
Through earth's labyrinth to guide me
  To a bright and heavenly land.

Hallelujah! I believe!
  Sorrow's bitterness is o'er,
And affliction's heavy burden
  Weighs my spirit down no more.
On the cross the mystic writing
  Now revealed before me lies,

And I read the words of comfort,
  "As a father, I chastise."

Hallelujah! I believe!
  Now no longer on my soul
All the debt of sin is lying:
  One great Friend has paid the whole!
Ice-bound fields of legal labor
  I have left with all their toil,
While the fruits of love are growing
  From a new and genial soil.

Hallelujah! I believe!
  Now life's mystery is gone;
Gladly through its fleeting shadows,
  To the end I journey on.
Through the tempest or the sunshine,
  Over flowers or ruins led,
Still the path is *homeward* hasting,
  Where all sorrow shall have fled.

Hallelujah! I believe!
  Now, O Love! I know Thy power,
Thine no false or fragile fetters,
  Not the rose-wreaths of an hour!
Christian bonds of holy union
  Death itself does not destroy;
Yes, to live and love forever,
  Is our heritage of joy!

*Heinrich Mowes.*
*Tr. by Miss Jane Borthwick.*

## IN THY SERVICE WILL I EVER.

In Thy service will I ever,
  Jesus, my Redeemer, stay;
Nothing me from Thee shall sever,
  Gladly would I go Thy way.
Life in me Thy life produces,
  And gives vigor to my heart,
As the vine doth living juices
  To the purple grape impart.

Could I be in other places
  Half so happy as with Thee,
Who so many gifts and graces
  Hast Thyself prepared for me?
No place could be half so fitted
  To impart true joy, I ween,
Since to Thee, O Lord! committed
  Power in heaven and earth hath been.

Where shall I find such a Master,
  Who hath done my soul such g⸺
And retrieved the great disaster
  Sin first caused, by His own '
Is not He my rightful owner,
  Who for me His own life ny plea:
Were it not a foul dishonor
  Not to love Him to the grave.

Yes, Lord Jesus, I am ever
  Thine in sorrow and in joy;

### 150 *In Thy Service will I ever.*

Death the union shall not sever,
  Nor eternity destroy.
I am waiting, yea, am sighing
  For my summons to depart;
He is best prepared for dying
  Who in life is Thine in heart.

Let Thy light on me be shining
  When the day is almost gone
When the evening is declining,
  And the night is drawing on:
Bless me, O my Saviour! laying
  Thy hands on my weary head;
" Here thy day is ended," saying,
  " Yonder live the faithful dead."

Stay beside me, when the stillness
  And the icy touch of death
Fills my trembling soul with chillness,
  Like the morning's frosty breath;
My failing eyes grow dimmer,
  Now my spirit grow more bright,
Thine is the first faint glimmer
  Not the everlasting light.

*Rev. Carl Johann Phillip Spitta.*
  *Tr. by Richard Massie.*

## LET THE WORLD THEIR VIRTUE BOAST

Let the world their virtue boast,
   Their works of righteousness;
I, a wretch undone and lost,
   Am freely saved by grace;
Other title I disclaim,
   This, only this, is all my plea;
I the chief of sinners am,
   But Jesus died for me.

Happy they whose joys abound
   Like Jordan's swelling stream,
Who their heaven in Christ have found;
   And give the praise to Him;
Meanest follower of the Lamb,
   His steps I at a distance see:
I the chief of sinners am,
   But Jesus died for me.

Jesus, Thou for me hast died,
   And Thou in me wilt live;
I shall feel Thy death applied;
   I shall Thy life receive;
Yet, when melted in the flame
   Of love, this shall be all my plea:
I the chief of sinners am,
   But Jesus died for me.

*Rev. Charles Wesley.* a/.

## O COULD I SPEAK!

O could I speak the matchless worth,
O could I sound the glories forth,
   Which in my Saviour shine,
I'd soar, and touch the heavenly strings,
And vie with Gabriel while he sings
   In notes almost divine.

I'd sing the precious blood He spilt,
My ransom from the dreadful guilt
   Of sin, and wrath divine;
I'd sing His glorious righteousness,
In which all-perfect, heavenly dress
   My soul shall ever shine.

I'd sing the characters He bears,
And all the forms of love He wears,
   Exalted on His throne;
In loftiest songs of sweetest praise,
I would to everlasting days
   Make all His glories known.

Well, the delightful day will come
When my dear Lord will bring me home,
   And I shall see His face;
Then with my Saviour, Brother, Friend,
A blest eternity I'll spend,
   Triumphant in His grace.

*Rev. Samuel Medley.* ab.

## COME, LET US JOIN.

Come, let us join our cheerful songs
    With angels round the throne;
Ten thousand thousand are their tongues,
    But all their joys are one.

"Worthy the Lamb that died," they cry,
    "To be exalted thus!"
"Worthy the Lamb!" our lips reply,
    "For He was slain for us."

Jesus is worthy to receive
    Honor and power divine;
And blessings more than we can give,
    Be, Lord, forever Thine!

Let all that dwell above the sky,
    And air and earth and seas,
Conspire to lift Thy glories high,
    And speak Thine endless praise.

The whole creation join in one,
    To bless the sacred name
Of Him who sits upon the throne,
    And to adore the Lamb!

*Rev. Isaac Watts.*

## O FOR A THOUSAND TONGUES!

O for a thousand tongues to sing
   My great Redeemer's praise!
The glories of my God and King,
   The triumphs of His grace!

My gracious Master and my God,
   Assist me to proclaim,
To spread through all the earth abroad,
   The honors of Thy name.

Jesus! the name that calms our fears,
   That bids our sorrows cease;
'Tis music in the sinner's ears;
   'Tis life and health and peace!

He breaks the power of cancelled sin;
   He sets the prisoner free;
His blood can make the foulest clean;
   His blood availed for me.

He speaks; and, listening to His voice,
   New life the dead receive;
The mournful, broken hearts rejoice;
   The humble poor believe.

Hear Him, ye deaf! His praise, ye dumb,
   Your loosened tongues employ!
Ye blind, behold your Saviour come;
   And leap, ye lame, for joy!

Look unto Him, ye nations! own
  Your God, ye fallen race!
Look, and be saved through faith alone,
  Be justified by grace!

See all your sins on Jesus laid:
  The Lamb of God was slain;
His soul was once an offering made
  For every soul of man.

Awake from guilty nature's sleep,
  And Christ shall give you light;
Cast all your sins into the deep,
  And wash the Ethiop white.

With Me, your chief, ye then shall know,
  Shall feel, your sins forgiven;
Anticipate your heaven below,
  And own that love is heaven.
            *Rev. Charles Wesley.*

---

AWAKE, AND SING THE SONG.

Awake, and sing the song
  Of Moses and the Lamb;
Tune every heart and every tongue,
  To praise the Saviour's name.

Sing of His dying love;
  Sing of His rising power;
Sing how He intercedes above
  For those whose sins He bore.

## 156 *Awake, and sing the Song.*

Tell, in seraphic strains,
  What Christ has done for you;
How He has taken off your chains,
  And formed your hearts anew.

Are you in deep distress?
  Then sing to ease the smart.
Are you rejoiced? let psalms express
  The gladness of your heart.

When Paul and Silas sung,
  The earth began to quake;
The prison doors were open flung,
  Her firm foundations shake.

Sing, till you feel your hearts
  Ascending with your tongues;
Sing, till the love of sin departs,
  And grace inspires your songs.

Sing on your heavenly way:
  Ye ransomed sinners, sing!
Sing on, rejoicing every day,
  Of Christ the eternal King.

Soon shall our raptured tongue
  In heaven His praise proclaim,
And sweeter voices tune the song
  Of Moses and the Lamb.

*Rev. William Hammond.*

## HAIL, THOU ONCE DESPISÈD JESUS!

Hail, Thou once despisèd Jesus!
  Hail, Thou Galilean King!
Who didst suffer to release us;
  Who didst free salvation bring:
Hail, Thou agonizing Saviour,
  Who hast borne our sin and shame!
By whose merits we find favor;
  Life is given through Thy name.

Paschal Lamb, by God appointed,
  All our sins were on Thee laid;
By almighty love appointed,
  Thou hast full atonement made:
Every sin may be forgiven
  Through the virtue of Thy blood;
Opened is the gate of heaven;
  Peace is made 'twixt man and God.

Jesus, hail! enthroned in glory,
  There forever to abide;
All the heavenly hosts adore Thee,
  Seated at Thy Father's side:
There for sinners Thou art pleading:
  There Thou dost our place prepare;
Ever for us interceding,
  Till in glory we appear.

Worship, honor, power, and blessing,
  Christ is worthy to receive;

## 158 *O had I, my Saviour!*

Loudest praises, without ceasing,
   Meet it is for us to give.
Help, ye bright angelic spirits!
   Bring your sweetest, noblest lays!
Help to sing our Jesu's merits;
   Help to chant Immanuel's praise.
*Rev. John Bakewell*

---

### O HAD I, MY SAVIOUR!

O had I, my Saviour, the wings of a dove,
How soon would I soar to Thy presence above;
How soon would I flee where the weary have rest,
And hide all my cares in Thy sheltering breast.

I flutter, I struggle, I pant to get free;
I feel me a captive while banished from Thee:
A pilgrim and stranger, the desert I roam,
And look on to heaven, and long to be home.

Ah, there the wild tempest forever shall cease;
No billow shall ruffle that haven of peace;
Temptation and trouble alike shall depart,
All tears from the eye, and all sin from the heart.

Soon, soon may this Eden of promise be
  mine;
Rise, bright Sun of glory, no more to decline:
Thy light, yet unrisen, the wilderness cheers;
O what will it be when the fulness appears?

*Rev. Henry Francis Lyte.*

## SUN OF MY SOUL.

Sun of my soul, Thou Saviour dear,
It is not night if Thou be near;
Oh! may no earth-born cloud arise
To hide Thee from Thy servant's eyes!

When round Thy wondrous works below
My searching rapturous glance I throw,
Tracing out wisdom, power, and love,
In earth or sky; in stream or grove;

Or, by the light Thy words disclose,
Watch time's full river as it flows,
Scanning Thy gracious providence,
Where not too deep for mortal sense;

When with dear friends sweet talk I hold,
And all the flowers of life unfold,—
Let not my heart within me burn,
Except in all I Thee discern!

When the soft dews of kindly sleep
My weared eyelids gently steep,

Be my last thought, how sweet to rest
Forever on my Saviour's breast !

Abide with me from morn till eve,
For without Thee I cannot live !
Abide with me when night is nigh,
For without Thee I dare not die !

Thou Framer of the light and dark,
Steer through the tempest Thine own ark !
Amid the howling wintry sea
We are in port if we have Thee.

The rulers of this Christian land,
'Twixt Thee and us ordained to stand,
Guide Thou their course, O Lord ! aright;
Let all do all as in Thy sight !

Oh ! by Thine own sad burthen, borne
So meekly up the hill of scorn,
Teach Thou Thy priests their daily cross
To bear as Thine, nor count it loss !

If some poor wandering child of Thine
Have spurned, to-day, the voice divine;
Now, Lord, the gracious work begin;
Let him no more lie down in sin !

Watch by the sick, enrich the poor
With blessings from Thy boundless store !
Be every mourner's sleep to-night
Like infant's slumbers, pure and light !

Come near and bless us when we wake,
Ere through the world our way we take:
Till, in the ocean of Thy love,
We lose ourselves in Heaven above!
*Rev. John Keble.*

---

## LORD, IT BELONGS NOT TO MY CARE.

Lord, it belongs not to my care
   Whether I die or live;
To love and serve Thee is my share,
   And this Thy grace must give.

If life be long I will be glad,
   That I may long obey;
If short, yet why should I be sad,
   To soar to endless day.

Christ leads me through no darker rooms
   Than He went through before;
He that unto God's kingdom comes
   Must enter by this door.

Come, Lord, when grace has made me meet
   Thy blessèd face to see;
For if Thy work on earth be sweet,
   What will Thy glory be!

Then shall I end my sad complaints,
   And weary, sinful days,
And join with the triumphant saints
   To sing Jehovah's praise.

My knowledge of that life is small,
  The eye of faith is dim;
But it's enough that Christ knows all,
  And I shall be with Him.
                    *Rev. Richard Baxter.*

---

## THAT MYSTIC WORD OF THINE.

That mystic word of Thine, O sovereign Lord,
  Is all too pure, too high, too deep for me;
Weary of striving, and with longing faint,
  I breathe it back again in *prayer* to Thee.

Abide in me, I pray, and I in Thee!
  From this good hour, O, leave me nevermore!
Then shall the discord cease, the wound be healed,
  The life-long bleeding of the soul be o'er.

Abide in me; o'ershadow by Thy love
  Each half-formed purpose and dark thought of sin;
Quench, e'er it rise, each selfish, low desire,
  And keep my soul as Thine, calm and divine.

As some rare perfume in a vase of clay
   Pervades it with a fragrance not its own,
So, when Thou dwellest in a mortal soul,
   All heaven's own sweetness seems around it thrown.

The soul alone, like a neglected harp,
   Grows out of tune, and needs that Hand divine:
Dwell Thou within it, tune and touch the chords,
   Till every note and string shall answer Thine.

Abide in me: there have been moments blest,
   When I have heard Thy voice and felt Thy power,
Then evil lost its grasp; and passion, hushed,
   Owned the divine enchantment of the hour.

These were but seasons, beautiful and rare;
   Abide in me, and they shall ever be;
Fulfil at once Thy precept and my prayer,
   Come, and abide in me, and I in Thee.

*Mrs. Harriet Beecher Stowe.*

## STAR OF PEACE.

Star of peace, to wanderers weary,
    Bright the beams that smile on me;
Cheer the pilot's vision dreary,
    Far, far at sea.

Star of hope, gleam on the billow,
    Bless the soul that sighs for thee;
Bless the sailor's lonely pillow,
    Far, far at sea.

Star of faith, when winds are mocking
    All his toil, he flies to thee;
Save him on the billows rocking,
    Far, far at sea.

Star divine, O safely guide him,
    Bring the wanderer home to thee:
Sore temptations long have tried him,
    Far, far at sea.
      *Mrs. Jane Cross Bell Simpson.* ab.

---

## WITH CEASELESS COURSE THE SUN.

While with ceaseless course the sun
    Hasted through the former year,
Many souls their race have run,
    Never more to meet us here:

Fixed in an eternal state,
   They have done with all below;
We a little longer wait,
   But how little none can know.

As the wingéd arrow flies
   Speedily the mark to find;
As the lightning from the skies
   Darts, and leaves no trace behind;
Swiftly thus our fleeting days
   Bear us down life's rapid stream:
Upward, Lord, our spirits raise,
   All below is but a dream.

Thanks for mercies past receive;
   Pardon of our sins renew;
Teach us henceforth how to live
   With eternity in view;
Bless Thy word to young and old;
   Fill us with a Saviour's love;
And when life's short tale is told,
   May we dwell with Thee above.

*Rev. John Newton.*

---

## SOFTLY NOW THE LIGHT OF DAY.

Softly now the light of day
Fades upon my sight away;
Free from care, from labor free,
Lord, I would commune with Thee.

Thou, whose all-pervading eye
Naught escapes, without, within,
Pardon each infirmity,
Open fault and secret sin.

Soon, for me, the light of day
Shall forever pass away:
Then, from sin and sorrow free,
Take me, Lord, to dwell with Thee.

Thou who, sinless, yet hast known
All of man's infirmity;
Then, from Thine eternal throne,
Jesus, look with pitying eye.
*Bp. George Washington Doane.*

---

## HAIL TO THE LORD'S ANOINTED.

Hail to the Lord's Anointed,
  Great David's greater Son;
Hail, in the time appointed,
  His reign on earth begun.
He comes to break oppression,
  To set the captive free;
To take away transgression,
  And rule in equity.

He comes with succor speedy
  To those who suffer wrong;
To help the poor and needy,
  And bid the weak be strong;

To give them songs for sighing,
   Their darkness turn to light,
Whose souls, condemned and dying,
   Were precious in His sight.

He shall come down like showers
   Upon the fruitful earth;
And love, joy, hope, like flowers,
   Spring in His path to birth:
Before Him on the mountains
   Shall peace, the herald, go;
And righteousness, in fountains,
   From hill to valley flow.

For Him shall prayer unceasing
   And daily vows ascend;
His kingdom still increasing,
   A kingdom without end:
The mountain dews shall nourish
   A seed in weakness sown,
Whose fruit shall spread, and flourish,
   And shake like Lebanon.

O'er every foe victorious
   He on His throne shall rest,
From age to age more glorious,
   All-blessing and all-blest;
The tide of time shall never
   His covenant remove;
His name shall stand forever,
   That name to us is Love.

          *James Montgomery. ab.*

## ONWARD, CHRISTIAN SOLDIERS.

Onward, Christian soldiers,
    Marching as to war,
With the Cross of Jesus
    Going on before.
Christ the Royal Master
    Leads against the foe,
Forward into battle,
    See, His banners go.
        Onward, Christian soldiers,
           Marching as to war,
        With the Cross of Jesus
           Going on before.

At the sign of triumph
    Satan's host doth flee;
On, then, Christian soldiers
    On to victory.
Hell's foundations quiver
    At the shout of praise;
Brothers, lift your voices,
    Loud your anthems raise.
            Onward, etc.

Like a mighty army
    Moves the Church of God;
Brothers, we are treading
    Where the saints have trod;

## Onward, Christian Soldiers.

We are not divided,
  All one body we,
One in hope and doctrine,
  One in charity.
        Onward, etc.

Crowns and thrones may perish,
  Kingdoms rise and wane,
But the Church of Jesus
  Constant will remain;
Gates of hell can never
  'Gainst that Church prevail;
We have Christ's own promise,
  And that cannot fail.
        Onward, etc.

Onward, then, ye people,
  Join our happy throng,
Blend with ours your voices,
  In the triumph song:
Glory, laud, and honor,
  Unto Christ the King.
This through countless ages
  Men and Angels sing.
        Onward, Christian soldiers,
          Marching as to war,
        With the Cross of Jesus
          Going on before.
        *Rev. Sabine Baring Gould.*

## FROM GREENLAND'S ICY MOUNTAINS

From Greenland's icy mountains,
   From India's coral strand,
Where Afric's sunny fountains
   Roll down their golden sand:
From many an ancient river,
   From many a palmy plain,
They call us to deliver
   Their land from error's chain.

What though the spicy breezes
   Blow soft o'er Ceylon's isle,
Though every prospect pleases,
   And only man is vile:
In vain with lavish kindness
   The gifts of God are strewn,
The heathen in his blindness
   Bows down to wood and stone.

Can we, whose souls are lighted
   With wisdom from on high,
Can we to men benighted
   The lamp of life deny?
Salvation, O Salvation!
   The joyful sound proclaim,
Till each remotest nation
   Has learnt Messiah's name.

Waft, waft, ye winds, His story,
   And you, ye waters, roll.
Till, like a sea of glory,
   It spreads from pole to pole:
Till o'er our ransomed nature,
   The Lamb for sinners slain,
Redeemer, King, Creator,
   In bliss returns to reign.

*Bp. Reginald Heber*

---

## FORWARD! BE OUR WATCHWORD.

Forward! be our watchword,
   Steps and voices joined;
Seek the things before us,
   Not a look behind:
Burns the fiery pillar
   At our army's head;
Who shall dream of shrinking,
   By our Captain led?
Forward through the desert,
   Through the toil and fight:
Jordan flows before us,
   Zion beams with light!

Forward, flock of Jesus,
   Salt of all the earth;
Till each yearning purpose
   Spring to glorious birth:

Sick, they ask for healing,
    Blind, they grope for day;
Pour upon the nations
    Wisdom's loving ray.
Forward, out of error,
    Leave behind the night;
Forward through the darkness,
    Forward into Light!

Glories upon glories
    Hath our God prepared,
By the souls that love Him
    One day to be shared:
Eye hath not beheld them,
    Ear hath never heard;
Nor of these hath uttered
    Thought or speech a word:
Forward, marching eastward
    Where the heaven is bright,
Till the veil be lifted,
    Till our faith be sight!

Far o'er yon horizon
    Rise the city towers,
Where our God abideth;
    That fair home is ours:
Flash the streets with jasper,
    Shine the gates with gold;
Flows the gladdening river
    Shedding joys untold;

Thither, onward thither,
  In the Spirit's might:
Forward into Triumph,
  Forward into Light.
*Rev. Henry Alford.*

## WATCHMAN! TELL US OF THE NIGHT.

Watchman! tell us of the night,
  What its signs of promise are.
Traveller! o'er yon mountain's height,
  See that glory-beaming star.

Watchman! does its beauteous ray
  Aught of hope or joy foretell?
Traveller! yes; it brings the day,
  Promised day of Israel.

Watchman! tell us of the night;
  Higher yet that star ascends.
Traveller! blessedness and light,
  Peace and truth, its course portends.

Watchman! will its beams alone
  Gild the spot that gave them birth?
Traveller! ages are its own;
  See, it bursts o'er all the earth!

Watchman! tell us of the night,
  For the morning seems to dawn.
Traveller! darkness takes its flight;
  Doubt and terror are withdrawn.

Watchman! let thy wanderings cease,
    Hie thee to thy quiet home:
Traveller! lo, the Prince of Peace,
    Lo, the Son of God, is come!
Sir John Bowring.

---

## LIGHT OF THOSE WHOSE DREARY.

Light of those whose dreary dwelling
    Borders on the shades of death,
Come, and by Thy love's revealing
    Dissipate the clouds beneath:
The new heaven and earth's Creator,
    In our deepest darkness rise,
Scattering all the night of nature,
    Pouring eye-sight on our eyes.

Still we wait for Thine appearing;
    Life and joy Thy beams impart,
Chasing all our fears, and cheering
    Every poor benighted heart:
Come, and manifest the favor
    God hath for our ransomed race;
Come, Thou glorious God and Saviour,
    Come, and bring the gospel-grace.

Save us in Thy great compassion,
    O Thou mild, pacific Prince,
Give the knowledge of salvation,
    Give the pardon of our sins;

By Thine all-restoring merit,
   Every burdened soul release,
Every weary, wandering spirit
   Guide into Thy perfect peace.
*Rev. Charles Wesley.*

---

### JESUS SHALL REIGN.

Jesus shall reign where'er the sun
Does his successive journeys run;
His kingdom stretch from shore to shore,
Till moons shall wax and wane no more.

Behold the islands with their kings,
And Europe her best tribute brings;
From north to south the princes meet
To pay their homage at His feet.

There Persia, glorious to behold,
There India shines in eastern gold;
And barb'rous nations, at His word,
Submit and bow, and own their Lord.

For Him shall endless prayer be made,
And praises throng to crown His head;
His name, like sweet perfume, shall rise
With every morning sacrifice.

People and realms of every tongue
Dwell on His love with sweetest song;
And infant voices shall proclaim
Their early blessings on His name.

Blessings abound where'er He reigns;
The prisoner leaps to lose his chains;
The weary find eternal rest,
And all the sons of want are blest.

Where He displays His healing power,
Death and the curse are known no more;
In Him the tribes of Adam boast
More blessings than their father lost.

Let every creature rise, and bring
Peculiar honors to our King;
Angels descend with songs again,
And earth repeat the long Amen!

*Rev. Isaac Watts.*

## BEHOLD THE GLORIES.

Behold the glories of the Lamb
   Amidst His Father's throne!
Prepare new honors for His name,
   And songs before unknown.

Let elders worship at His feet,
   The Church adore around,
With vials full of odors sweet,
   And harps of sweeter sound.

Those are the prayers of the saints,
   And these the hymns they raise;
Jesus is kind to our complaints,
   He loves to hear our praise.

Eternal Father, who shall look
  Into Thy secret will?
Who but the Son should take that book,
  And open every seal?

He shall fulfil Thy great decrees:
  The Son deserves it well;
Lo, in His hand the sov'reign keys
  Of heaven and death and hell!

Now to the Lamb, that once was slain,
  Be endless blessings paid;
Salvation, glory, joy, remain
  Forever on Thy head.

Thou hast redeemed our souls with blood,
  Hast set the prisoners free,
Hast made us kings and priests to God,
  And we shall reign with Thee.

The worlds of nature and of grace
  Are put beneath Thy power;
Then shorten these delaying days,
  And bring the promised hour.
                    *Rev. Isaac Watts.*

---

## A FEW MORE YEARS.

A few more years shall roll,
  A few more seasons come,
And we shall be with those that rest
  Asleep within the tomb.

## A few more Years.

A few more suns shall set
   O'er these dark hills of time;
And we shall be where suns are not,
   A far serener clime.

A few more storms shall beat
   On this wild, rocky shore;
And we shall be where tempests cease,
   And surges swell no more.

A few more struggles here,
   A few more partings o'er,
A few more toils, a few more tears,
   And we shall weep no more.

A few more Sabbaths here
   Shall cheer us on our way;
And we shall reach the endless rest,
   The eternal Sabbath day.

'Tis but a little while,
   And He shall come again,
Who died that we might live, who lives
   That we with Him may reign.

Then O, my Lord, prepare
   My soul for that glad day;
O wash me in Thy precious blood,
   And take my sins away.
              *Rev. Horatius Bonar.* ab.

## WHEN LANGUOR AND DISEASE.

When languor and disease invade
   This trembling house of clay,
'Tis sweet to look beyond the cage,
   And long to fly away.

Sweet to look inward, and attend
   The whispers of His love;
Sweet to look upward to the place
   Where Jesus pleads above;

Sweet to look back, and see my name
   In life's fair book set down;
Sweet to look forward, and behold
   Eternal joys my own;

Sweet on His faithfulness to rest,
   Whose love can never end;
Sweet on His covenant of grace
   For all things to depend;

Sweet, in the confidence of faith,
   To trust His firm decrees;
Sweet to lie passive in His hands,
   And know no will but His;

Sweet to rejoice in lively hope,
   That, when my change shall come,
Angels will hover round my bed,
   And waft my spirit home.

If such the sweetness of the streams,
  What must the fountain be,
Where saints and angels draw their bliss,
  Immediately from Thee!
        *Rev. Augustus Toplady. ab.*

---

### THOU ART GONE.

Thou art gone to the grave; but we will not deplore thee,
  Though sorrows and darkness encompass the tomb;
Thy Saviour has passed through the portal before thee,
  And the lamp of His love is thy guide through the gloom.

Thou art gone to the grave; we no longer behold thee,
  Nor tread the rough path of the world by thy side:
But the wide arms of mercy are spread to enfold thee,
  And sinners may die, for the Sinless hath died.

Thou art gone to the grave; and, its mansion forsaking,
  Perchance thy weak spirit in fear lingered long;

But the mild rays of Paradise beamed on
    thy waking,
  And the sound which thou heard'st was
    the seraphim's song.

Thou art gone to the grave; but we will not
    deplore thee,
  Whose God was thy Ransom, thy Guardian and Guide:
He gave thee, He took thee, and He will
    restore thee;
  And death has no sting, for the Saviour
    has died.

*Bp. Reginald Heber.*

## YE GOLDEN LAMPS OF HEAVEN.

Ye golden lamps of heaven, farewell,
  With all your feeble light;
Farewell, thou ever changing moon,
  Pale empress of the night.

And thou, refulgent orb of day,
  In brighter flames arrayed;
My soul, that springs beyond thy sphere,
  No more demands thine aid.

Ye stars are but the shining dust
  Of my divine abode,
The pavement of those heavenly courts
  Where I shall reign with God.

The Father of eternal light
  Shall there His beams display,
Nor shall one moment's darkness mix
  With that unvaried day.

No more the drops of piercing grief
  Shall swell into mine eyes;
Nor the meridian sun decline
  Amid those brighter skies.

There all the millions of His saints
  Shall in one song unite,
And each the bliss of all shall view
  With infinite delight.

*Rev. Philip Doddridge*

---

### REJOICE, ALL YE BELIEVERS.

Rejoice, all ye believers,
  And let your lights appear!
The evening is advancing,
  And darker night is near:
The Bridegroom is arising,
  And soon will He draw nigh.
Up! pray and watch and wrestle:
  At midnight comes the cry.

See that your lamps are burning,
  Replenish them with oil;
Look now for your salvation,
  **The end of earthly toil.**

## Rejoice, all ye Believers.

The watchers on the mountain
   Proclaim the Bridegroom near;
Go meet Him as He cometh,
   With Hallelujahs clear!

Ye wise and holy virgins,
   Now raise your voices higher,
Until, in songs of triumph,
   They meet the angel-choir.
The marriage-feast is waiting,
   The gates wide open stand;
Up! up! ye heirs of glory:
   The Bridegroom is at hand!

Ye saints who here in patience
   Your cross and sufferings bore,
Shall live and reign forever,
   When sorrow is no more.
Around the throne of glory,
   The Lamb ye shall behold;
In triumph cast before Him
   Your diadems of gold!

There flourish palms of victory;
   There radiant garments are;
There stands the peaceful harvest,
   Beyond the reach of war.
There, after stormy winter,
   The flowers of earth arise,
And from the grave's long slumber
   Shall meet again our eyes.

Our Hope and Expectation,
  O Jesus! now appear;
Arise, Thou Sun, so longed for,
  O'er this benighted sphere!
With hearts and hands uplifted,
  We plead, O Lord! to see
The day of our redemption,
  That brings us unto Thee!
            *Laurentius Laurenti.*
      *Tr. by Miss Jane Borthwick.*

---

## LO! HE COMES.

Lo! He comes with clouds descending,
  Once for favored sinners slain!
Thousand, thousand saints attending,
  Swell the triumph of His train:
    Hallelujah!
  God appears on earth to reign!

Every eye shall now behold Him
  Robed in dreadful majesty;
Those who set at nought and sold Him,
  Pierced, and nailed Him to the tree,
    Deeply wailing,
  Shall the true Messiah see.

Every island, sea, and mountain,
  Heaven and earth, shall flee away;
All who hate Him must, confounded,

Hear the trump proclaim the day:
  Come to judgment!
Come to judgment, come away!

Now redemption, long expected,
  See in solemn pomp appear!
All His saints, by man rejected,
  Now shall meet Him in the air:
    Hallelujah!
  See the day of God appear.

The dear tokens of His passion
  Still His dazzling body bears,
Cause of endless exultation
  To His ransomed worshippers;
    With what rapture
  Gaze we on those glorious scars!

Yea, Amen! let all adore Thee,
  High on Thine eternal throne!
Saviour, take the power and glory,
  Claim the kingdom for Thine own:
    O come quickly!
  Hallelujah, come, Lord, come.

*Rev. Charles Wesley*
*Rev. Martin Madan*

## BEHOLD, THE BRIDEGROOM COMETH.

Behold, the Bridegroom cometh in the middle of the night,
And blest is he whose loins are girt, whose lamp is burning bright;
But woe to that dull servant, whom the Master shall surprise
With lamp untrimmed, unburning, and with slumber in his eyes.

Do thou, my soul, beware, beware lest thou in sleep sink down,
Lest thou be given o'er to death, and lose the golden crown;
But see that thou be sober, with watchful eye, and thus
Cry, "Holy, holy, holy God, have mercy upon us."

That day, the day of fear, shall come; my soul slack not thy toil,
But light thy lamp, and feed it well, and make it bright with oil;
Who knowest not how soon may sound the cry at eventide,
"Behold the Bridegroom comes. Arise! Go forth to meet the Bride."

Beware, my soul, take thou good heed, lest
    thou in slumber lie,
And, like the five, remain without, and
    knock, and vainly cry;
But watch, and bear thy lamp undimmed,
    and Christ shall gird thee on
His own bright wedding-robe of light, the
    glory of the Son.

*Rev. Gerard Moultrie*

---

### ASLEEP IN JESUS.

Asleep in Jesus! blessèd sleep,
From which none ever wakes to weep,
A calm and undisturbed repose,
Unbroken by the last of foes!

Asleep in Jesus! oh, how sweet
To be for such a slumber meet!
With holy confidence to sing
That death hath lost his venomed sting.

Asleep in Jesus! peaceful rest,
Whose waking is supremely blest;
No fear, no woe, shall dim that hour,
That manifests the Saviour's power.

Asleep in Jesus! oh for me
May such a blissful refuge be;
Securely shall my ashes lie,
Waiting the summons from on high!

Asleep in Jesus! time nor space
Debars this precious "hiding-place;"
On Indian plains, or Lapland snows,
Believers find the same repose.

Asleep in Jesus! far from thee
Thy kindred and their graves may be;
But thine is still a blessèd sleep,
From which none ever wakes to weep!
*Mrs. Margaret Mackay*

---

### NO, NO, IT IS NOT DYING.

No, no, it is not dying,
To go unto our God;
This gloomy earth forsaking,
Our journey homeward taking
Along the starry road.

No, no, it is not dying,
Heaven's citizen to be;
A crown immortal wearing,
And rest unbroken sharing,
From care and conflict free

No, no, it is not dying,
To hear this gracious word:
" Receive a Father's blessing,
For evermore possessing
The favor of thy Lord."

No, no, it is not dying,
  The Shepherd's voice to know;
His sheep He ever leadeth,
His peaceful flock He feedeth,
  Where living pastures grow.

No, no, it is not dying,
  To wear a lordly crown;
Among God's people dwelling,
The glorious triumph swelling,
  Of Him whose sway we own.

Oh, no, this is not dying,
  Thou Saviour of mankind!
There streams of love are flowing,
No hindrance ever knowing;
  Here drops alone we find.

*Rev. Cæsar Malan.*
*Tr. by Rev. R. P. Dunn.*

---

## THERE IS A BLESSED HOME.

There is a blessèd home
  Beyond this land of woe,
Where trials never come,
  Nor tears of sorrow flow;
Where faith is lost in sight,
  And patient hope is crowned,
And everlasting light
  Its glory throws around.

## There is a blessed Home.

There is a land of peace,
   Good angels know it well;
Glad songs that never cease
   Within its portals swell;
Around its glorious throne
   Ten thousand saints adore
Christ, with the Father One,
   And Spirit, evermore.

O joy all joys beyond,
   To see the Lamb who died,
And count each sacred wound
   In hands and feet and side!
To give to Him the praise
   Of every triumph won,
And sing through endless days
   The great things He hath done.

Look up, ye saints of God,
   Nor fear to tread below
The path your Saviour trod
   Of daily toil and woe;
Wait but a little while
   In uncomplaining love,
His own most gracious smile
   Shall welcome you above.
       *Rev. Sir Henry Williams Baker*

## FOREVER WITH THE LORD.

Forever with the Lord:
   Amen, so let it be;
Life from the dead is in that word,
   'Tis immortality.

Here in the body pent
   Absent from Him I roam,
Yet nightly pitch my moving tent
   A day's march nearer home.

My Father's house on high,
   Home of my soul, how near,
At times, to faith's far-seeing eye,
   Thy golden gates appear.

Ah, then my spirit faints
   To reach the land I love,
The bright inheritance of saints,
   Jerusalem above.

Yet clouds will intervene,
   And all my prospect flies,
Like Noah's dove I flit between
   Rough seas and stormy skies.

"Forever with the Lord:"
   Father, if 'tis Thy will,
The promise of that faithful word
   E'en here to me fulfil.

Anon the clouds depart,
  The winds and waters cease,
And sweetly o'er my gladdened heart
  Expands the bow of peace.
              *James Montgomery.*

---

### FOR ALL THE SAINTS.

For all the saints, who from their labors **rest**,
Who Thee by faith before the world confest,
Thy name, O Jesus, be forever blest,
                    Alleluia!

Thou wast their Rock, their Fortress and
    their Light;
Thou, Lord, their Captain in the well-fought
    fight;
Thou, in the darkness drear, their Light of
    light.
                    Alleluia!

O may Thy soldiers, faithful, true, and bold,
Fight as the saints who nobly fought of old,
And win with them the victor's crown of
    gold.
                    Alleluia!

O blest Communion, fellowship divine!
We feebly struggle, they in glory shine;
Yet all are one in Thee, for all are Thine.
                    Alleluia!

And when the strife is fierce, the warfare long,
Steals on the ear the distant triumph-song,
And hearts are brave again, and arms are strong.
       Alleluia!

The golden evening brightens in the west;
Soon, soon to faithful warriors comes the rest;
Sweet is the calm of Paradise the blest.
       Alleluia!

But lo, there breaks a yet more glorious day;
The saints triumphant rise in bright array;
The King of Glory passes on His way.
       Alleluia!

From earth's wide bounds, from ocean's farthest coast,
Through gates of pearl streams in the countless host,
Singing to Father, Son, and Holy Ghost.
       Alleluia!
   *Bp. William Walsham How.*

## THERE IS A LAND.

There is a land of pure delight,
 Where saints immortal reign,
Infinite day excludes the night,
 And pleasures banish pain,

## O Paradise, O Paradise!

There, everlasting springs abide,
 And never-withering flowers:
Death, like a narrow sea, divides
 This heavenly land from ours.

Sweet fields beyond the swelling flood,
 Stand dressed in living green:
So to the Jews old Canaan stood,
 While Jordan rolled between.
But timorous mortals start and shrink
 To cross this narrow sea,
And linger shivering on the brink,
 And fear to launch away.

O could we make our doubts remove
 Those gloomy doubts that rise,
And see the Canaan that we love
 With unbeclouded eyes:
Could we but climb where Moses stood,
 And view the landscape o'er,
Not Jordan's stream, nor death's cold flood,
 Should fright us from the shore.

*Rev. Isaac Watts.*

---

### O PARADISE, O PARADISE!

O Paradise, O Paradise,
 Who doth not crave for rest?
Who would not seek the happy land
 Where they that loved are blest?

## O Paradise, O Paradise!

    Where loyal hearts and true
      Stand ever in the light,
    All rapture through and through,
      In God's most holy sight.

O Paradise, O Paradise,
  The world is growing old;
Who would not be at rest and free
  Where love is never cold?
    Where loyal hearts and true
      Stand ever in the light,
    All rapture through and through,
      In God's most holy sight.

O Paradise, O Paradise,
  'Tis weary waiting here;
I long to be where Jesus is,
  To feel, to see Him near;
    Where loyal hearts and true
      Stand ever in the light,
    All rapture through and through,
      In God's most holy sight.

O Paradise, O Paradise,
  I want to sin no more,
I want to be as pure on earth
  As on thy spotless shore;
    Where loyal hearts and true
      Stand ever in the light,
    All rapture through and through,
      In God's most holy sight.

## 196 *Jerusalem, my happy Home.*

O Paradise, O Paradise,
  I greatly long to see
The special place my dearest Lord
  In love prepares for me;
    Where loyal hearts and true
      Stand ever in the light,
    All rapture through and through,
      In God's most holy sight.

Lord Jesu, King of Paradise,
  O keep me in Thy love,
And guide me to that happy land
  Of perfect rest above;
    Where loyal hearts and true
      Stand ever in the light,
    All rapture through and through,
      In God's most holy sight.
        *Rev. Frederick William Faber.*

---

### JERUSALEM, MY HAPPY HOME.

Jerusalem, my happy home,
  Name ever dear to me,
When shall my labors have an end
  In joy, and peace, and thee?

When shall these eyes thy heaven-built walls
  And pearly gates behold;
Thy bulwarks with salvation strong,
  And streets of shining gold?

O when, thou City of my God,
  Shall I thy courts ascend,
Where congregations ne'er break up,
  And Sabbaths have no end?

There happier bowers than Eden's bloom,
  Nor sin nor sorrow know:
Blest seats, through rude and stormy scenes
  I onward press to you.

Apostles, martyrs, prophets, there
  Around my Saviour stand;
And soon my friends in Christ below
  Will join the glorious band.

Jerusalem, my happy home,
  My soul still pants for thee;
Then shall my labors have an end
  When I thy joys shall see.
                    *Author Unknown.*

---

**TEN THOUSAND TIMES TEN THOUSAND**

  Ten thousand times ten thousand,
    In sparkling raiment bright,
  The armies of the ransomed saints
    Throng up the steeps of light:
  'Tis finished, all is finished,
    Their fight with death and sin:

## 198 *Who are these in bright Array.*

Fling open wide the golden gates,
  And let the victors in.

What rush of Hallelujahs
  Fills all the earth and sky;
What ringing of a thousand harps
  Bespeaks the triumph nigh.
O day, for which Creation
  And all its tribes were made;
O joy, for all its former woes
  A thousand-fold repaid.

O then what raptured greetings
  On Canaan's happy shore;
What knitting severed friendships up,
  Where partings are no more.
Then eyes with joy shall sparkle,
  That brimmed with tears of late:
Orphans no longer fatherless,
  Nor widows desolate.
         *Rev. Henry Alford.*

---

### WHO ARE THESE IN BRIGHT ARRAY

Who are these in bright array,
  This innumerable throng,
Round the altar night and day,
  Hymning one triumphant song:

"Worthy is the Lamb once slain,
 Blessing, honor, glory, power,
Wisdom, riches, to obtain,
 New dominion every hour."

These through fiery trials trod;
 These from great afflictions came;
Now, before the throne of God,
 Sealed with His Almighty Name;
Clad in raiment pure and white,
 Victor-palms in every hand,
Through their dear Redeemer's might,
 More than conquerors they stand.

Hunger, thirst, disease unknown,
 On immortal fruits they feed;
Them the Lamb amidst the throne,
 Shall to living fountains lead;
Joy and gladness banish sighs,
 Perfect love dispels their fears,
And forever from their eyes
 God shall wipe away their tears.

*James Montgomery*

## THE CELESTIAL COUNTRY.

The world is very evil,
    The times are waxing late;
Be sober and keep vigil,
    The Judge is at the gate—
The Judge that comes in mercy,
    The Judge that comes with might,
To terminate the evil,
    To diadem the right.
When the just and gentle Monarch
    Shall summon from the tomb,
Let man, the guilty, tremble,
    For Man, the God, shall doom!
Arise, arise, good Christian,
    Let right to wrong succeed;
Let penitential sorrow
    To heavenly gladness lead;
To the light that hath no evening,
    That knows nor moon nor sun,
The light so new and golden,
    The light that is but one.
And when the Sole-Begotten
    Shall render up once more
The Kingdom to the Father,
    Whose own it was before,—
Then glory yet unheard of
    Shall shed abroad its ray,
Resolving all enigmas,
    An endless Sabbath-day.

Then, then from his oppressors
   The Hebrew shall go free,
And celebrate in triumph
   The year of Jubilee;
And the sunlit Land that recks not
   Of tempest nor of fight,
Shall fold within its bosom
   Each happy Israelite:
The Home of fadeless splendor,
   Of flowers that fear no thorn,
Where they shall dwell as children,
   Who here as exiles mourn.
Midst power that knows no limit,
   And wisdom free from bound,
The Beatific Vision
   Shall glad the saints around:
The peace of all the faithful,
   The calm of all the blest,
Inviolate, unvaried,
   Divinest, sweetest, best.

Yes, Peace! for war is needless,—
   Yes, calm! for storm is past,—
And goal from finished labor,
   And anchorage at last.
That peace—but who may claim it?
   The guileless in their way,
Who keep the ranks of battle,
   Who mean the thing they say:

The peace that is for heaven,
  And shall be too, for earth:
The palace that re-echoes
  With festal song and mirth;
The garden, breathing spices,
  The paradise on high;
Grace beautified to glory,
  Unceasing minstrelsy.
There nothing can be feeble,
  There none can ever mourn,
There nothing is divided,
  There nothing can be torn.
'Tis fury, ill, and scandal,
  'Tis peaceless peace below;
Peace, endless, strifeless, ageless,
  The halls of Syon know.
O happy, holy portion,
  Refection for the blest;
True vision of true beauty,
  Sweet cure of all distrest!

Strive, man, to win that glory,
  Toil, man, to gain that light;
Send hope before to grasp it,
  Till hope be lost in sight:
Till Jesus gives the portion
  Those blessed souls to fill,
The insatiate, yet satisfied,
  The full, yet craving still.

That fulness and that craving
   Alike are free from pain,
Where thou, midst heavenly citizens,
   A home like theirs shall gain.
Here is the warlike trumpet;
   There, life set free from sin;
When to the last Great Supper
   The faithful shall come in:
When the heavenly net is laden
   With fishes many and great;
So glorious in its fulness,
   Yet so inviolate:
And the perfect from the shattered,
   And the fall'n from them that stand,
And the sheep-flock from the goat-herd
   Shall part on either hand:
And these shall pass to torment,
   And those shall pass to rest;
The new peculiar nation,
   The fulness of the Blest.

Jerusalem demands them:
   They paid the price on earth,
And now shall reap the harvest
   In blissfulness and mirth:
The glorious holy people,
   Who evermore relied
Upon their Chief and Father,
   The King, the Crucified:

The sacred ransomed number
  Now bright with endless sheen,
Who made the Cross their watchword
  Of Jesus Nazarene:
Who, fed with heavenly nectar,
  Where soul-like odors play,
Draw out the endless leisure
  Of that long vernal day:
While through the sacred lilies,
  And flowers on every side,
The happy dear-bought nations
  Go wandering far and wide.
Their breasts are filled with gladness,
  Their mouths are tuned to praise,
What time, now safe forever,
  On former sins they gaze:
The fouler was the error,
  The sadder was the fall,
The ampler are the praises
  Of Him who pardoned all.
Their one and only anthem,
  The fulness of His love,
Who gives instead of torment,
  Eternal joys above:
Instead of torment, glory;
  Instead of death, that life
Wherewith your happy Country,
  True Israelites! is rife.

## The celestial Country.

Brief life is here our portion;
   Brief sorrow, short-lived care:
The life that knows no ending,
   The tearless life, is *There*.
O happy retribution!
   Short toil, eternal rest;
For mortals and for sinners
   A mansion with the blest!
That we should look, poor wand'rers,
   To have our home on high!
That worms should seek for dwellings
   Beyond the starry sky!
To all one happy guerdon
   Of one celestial grace;
For all, for all, who mourn their fall,
   Is one eternal place:
And martyrdom hath roses
   Upon that heavenly ground:
And white and virgin lilies
   For virgin-souls abound.
There grief is turned to pleasure:
   Such pleasure, as below
No human voice can utter,
   No human heart can know.
And after fleshly scandal,
   And after this world's night,
And after storm and whirlwind
   Is calm, and joy, and light.

And now we fight the battle,
  But then shall wear the crown
Of full and everlasting
  And passionless renown:
And now we watch and struggle
  And now we live in hope,
And Syon, in her anguish,
  With Babylon must cope:
But He Whom now we trust in
  Shall then be seen and known,
And they that know and see Him
  Shall have Him for their own.
The miserable pleasures
  Of the body shall decay:
The bland and flattering struggles
  Of the flesh shall pass away:
And none shall there be jealous;
  And none shall there contend:
Fraud, clamor, guile—what say I?—
  All ill, all ill shall end!
And there is David's Fountain,
  And life in fullest glow,
And there the light is golden,
  And milk and honey flow:
The light that hath no evening,
  The health that hath no sore,
The life that hath no ending,
  But lasteth evermore.

There Jesus shall embrace us,
   There Jesus be embraced,—
That spirit's food and sunshine
   Whence meaner love is chased.
Amidst the happy chorus,
   A place, however low,
Shall show Him us; and showing,
   Shall satiate evermo.
By hope we struggle onward,
   While here we must be fed
With milk, as tender infants,
   But there with Living Bread.

The night was full of terror,
   The morn is bright with gladness:
The Cross becomes our harbor,
   And we triumph after sadness:
And Jesus to His true ones
   Brings trophies fair to see:
And Jesus shall be loved, and
   Beheld in Galilee.
Beheld, when morn shall waken,
   And shadows shall decay,
And each true-hearted servant
   Shall shine as doth the day:
And every ear shall hear it;—
   Behold thy King's array;
Behold thy God in beauty;
   The Law hath passed away!

Yes! God, my King and Portion,
  In fulness of His grace,
We then shall see forever,
  And worship face to face.

Then Jacob into Israel,
  From earthlier self estranged,
And Leah into Rachel
  Forever shall be changed:
Then all the halls of Syon
  For aye shall be complete;
And, in the Land of Beauty,
  All things of beauty meet.

For thee, O dear, dear Country!
  Mine eyes their vigils keep;
For very love, beholding
  Thy happy name, they weep:
The mention of thy glory
  Is unction to the breast,
And medicine in sickness,
  And love, and life, and rest.
O one, O onely Mansion!
  O Paradise of Joy!
Where tears are ever banished,
  And smiles have no alloy;
Beside thy living waters
  All plants are, great and small;
The cedar of the forest,
  The hyssop of the wall:

With jaspers glow thy bulwarks;
  Thy streets with emeralds blaze;
The sardius and the topaz
  Unite in thee their rays:
Thine ageless walls are bounded
  With amethyst unpriced:
Thy saints build up its fabric,
  And the corner-stone is Christ.

The Cross is all thy splendor,
  The Crucified thy praise:
His laud and benediction
  Thy ransomed people raise;
Jesus, the Gem of Beauty,
  True God and Man, they sing;
The never-failing Garden,
  The ever-golden Ring:
The Door, the Pledge, the Husband,
  The Guardian of His Court;
The Day-star of Salvation,
  The Porter and the Port;
Thou hast no shore, fair ocean!
  Thou hast no time, bright day!
Dear fountain of refreshment
  To pilgrims far away!
Upon the Rock of Ages
  They raise thy holy tower:
Thine is the victor's laurel,
  And thine the golden dower:

Thou feel'st in mystic rapture,
   O Bride, that knowest no guile,
The Prince's sweetest kisses,
   The Prince's loveliest smile:
Unfading lilies, bracelets
   Of living pearl, thine own;
The Lamb is ever near thee,
   The Bridegroom thine alone:
The Crown is He to guerdon,
   The Buckler to protect,
And He Himself the Mansion,
   And He the Architect.
The only art thou needest,
   Thanksgiving for thy lot:
The only joy thou seekest,
   The Life where Death is not.
And all thine endless leisure
   In sweetest accents sings,
The ill that was thy merit,—
   The wealth that is thy King's!

Jerusalem the Golden,
   With milk and honey blest,
Beneath thy contemplation
   Sink heart and voice oppressed:

I know not, O, I know not,
   What social joys are there;
What radiancy of glory,
   What light beyond compare!

And when I fain would sing them,
  My spirit fails and faints,—
And vainly would it image
  The assembly of the Saints.

They stand, those halls of Syon,
  Conjubilant with song,
And bright with many an angel,
  And all the martyr throng:

The Prince is ever in them;
  The daylight is serene;
The pastures of the blessed
  Are decked in glorious sheen.

There is the throne of David,—
  And there, from care released,
The song of them that triumph,
  The shout of them that feast;

And they who, with their Leader,
  Have conquered in the fight,
Forever and forever
  Are clad in robes of white.

O holy, placid harp-notes
  Of that eternal hymn!
O sacred sweet reflection,
  And peace of Seraphim!

O thirst, forever ardent,
  Yet evermore content!
O true, peculiar vision
  Of God cunctipotent!
Ye know the many mansions
  For many a glorious name,
And divers retributions
  That divers merits claim:
For midst the constellations
  That deck our earthly sky,
This star than that is brighter,—
  And so it is on high.

Jerusalem the glorious!
  The glory of the Elect!
O dear and future vision
  That eager hearts expect:
Even now by faith I see thee:
  Even here thy walls discern:
To thee my thoughts are kindled,
  And strive and pant and yearn:
Jerusalem the onely,
  That look'st from heaven below
In thee is all my glory;
  In me is all my woe;
And though my body may not,
  My spirit seeks thee fain,
Till flesh and earth return me
  To earth and flesh again.

Oh, none can tell thy bulwarks,
  How gloriously they rise:
Oh, none can tell thy capitals
  Of beautiful device:
Thy loveliness oppresses
  All human thought and heart:
And none, O peace, O Syon,
  Can sing thee as thou art.

New mansion of new people,
  Whom God's own love and light
Promote, increase, make holy,
  Identify, unite.
Thou City of the Angels!
  Thou City of the Lord!
Whose everlasting music
  Is the glorious decachord!
And there the band of Prophets
  United praise ascribes,
And there the twelvefold chorus
  Of Israel's ransomed tribes:
The lily-beds of virgins,
  The roses' martyr-glow,
The cohort of the Fathers
  Who kept the faith below.
And there the Sole-Begotten
  Is Lord in regal state;
He, Judah's mystic Lion,
  He, Lamb Immaculate.

## The celestial Country.

O fields that know no sorrow!
　O state that fears no strife!
O princely bow'rs! O land of flow'rs!
　O Realm and Home of Life!

Jerusalem, exulting
　On that securest shore,
I hope thee, wish thee, sing thee,
　And love thee evermore!
I ask not for my merit:
　I seek not to deny
My merit is destruction,
　A child of wrath am I:
But yet with Faith I venture
　And Hope upon my way;
For those perennial guerdons
　I labor night and day.
The Best and Dearest Father
　Who made me and Who saved,
Bore with me in defilement,
　And from defilement laved:
When in His strength I struggle,
　For very joy I leap;
When in my sin I totter,
　I weep, or try to weep:
And grace, sweet grace celestial,
　Shall all its love display,
And David's Royal Fountain
　Purge every sin away.

## The celestial Country.

O mine, my golden Syon!
  O lovelier far than gold!
With laurel-girt battalions,
  And safe victorious fold:
O sweet and blessed Country,
  Shall I ever see thy face!
O sweet and blessed Country,
  Shall I ever will thy grace?
I *have* the hope within me
  To comfort and to bless!
Shall I ever win the prize itself?
  O tell me, tell me, yes!
Exult, O dust and ashes!
  The Lord shall be thy part;
His only, His forever,
  Thou shalt be, and thou art!
Exult, O dust and ashes!
  The Lord shall be thy part:
His only, His forever,
  Thou shalt be, and thou art!

*Bernard of Cluny.*
*Tr. by Rev. John Mason Neale.*

## GLORY BE TO GOD THE FATHER!

Glory be to God the Father!
  Glory be to God the Son!
Glory be to God the Spirit!
  Great Jehovah, Three in One!
    Glory, glory,
  While eternal ages run!

Glory be to Him who loved us,
  Washed us from each spot and stain!
Glory be to Him who bought us,
  Made us kings with Him to reign!
    Glory, glory
  To the Lamb that once was slain!

Glory to the King of angels!
  Glory to the Church's King!
Glory to the King of nations!
  Heaven and earth your praises bring,—
    Glory, glory
  To the King of glory bring!

Glory, blessing, praise eternal!
  Thus the choir of angels sings;
Honor, riches, power, dominion!
  Thus its praise creation brings;
    Glory, glory,
  Glory to the King of kings!

*Rev. Horatius Bonar.*

# INDEX TO FIRST LINES.

Abide with me! fast falls the eventide......... 139
A few more years shall roll................... 177
Alas! and did my Saviour bleed?.............. 50
All hail the power of Jesus' name!............ 78
All my heart this night rejoices ............. 41
Amid life's wild commotion................... 135
Art thou weary, art thou languid?............ 125
A safe stronghold our God is still............ 1
Asleep in Jesus! blessèd sleep................ 187
As pants the hart for cooling streams......... 7
At the cross her station keeping............. 48
Awake, and sing the song..................... 155
Awake, my soul, and with the sun............ 36
Awake, my soul, in joyful lays............... 90

Behold, the Bridegroom cometh............... 186
Behold the glories of the Lamb............... 176
Brightest and best of the sons of the morning.. 39

Christ, the life of all the living.............. 55
Cling to the Crucified!...................... 122
Come, Holy Spirit, heavenly Dove........... 31
Come, let us join our cheerful songs.......... 153
Come, my soul, thy suit prepare............. 32

## Index to first Lines.

Come, thou Fount of every blessing.......... 26
Come, ye disconsolate, where'er ye languish... 19
Come, ye faithful, raise the strain........ .... 71

Fairest Lord Jesus............................ 89
Fierce was the wild billow.................... 124
For all the saints, who from their labors rest... 192
Forever with the Lord........................ 191
Forward! be our watchword................... 171
From every stormy wind that blows.......... 118
From Greenland's icy mountains.............. 170

Glory be to God the Father!.................. 216
Glory, my God, to Thee this night............ 38
God moves in a mysterious way.............. 3
Guide me, O Thou Great Jehovah............ 11

Hail, Thou once despisèd Jesus........... .... 157
Hail to the Lord's Anointed................... 166
Hallelujah! hallelujah!....................... 67
Hallelujah! I believe!........................ 147
Hark! the voice of love and mercy........... 60
Hark! what mean those holy voices........... 44
He is gone; beyond the skies.................. 75
Holy, holy, holy! Lord God Almighty...... . 8
Holy Spirit, Lord of light.................... 25
How firm a foundation....................... 6
How sweet the name of Jesus sounds.......... 110

If only I have Thee.......................... 143
I heard the voice of Jesus say................. 133
I know in whom I put my trust.............. 145
I know that my Redeemer lives.............. 81
I lay my sins on Jesus........................ 123
I need Thee, precious Jesus................... 115
In the cross of Christ I glory................. 61

## Index to first Lines.

In the silent midnight watches.............. 108
In Thy service will I ever.................. 149
It came upon the midnight clear............ 47
I was a wandering sheep.................... 113
I would not live alway; I ask not to stay...... 140

Jerusalem, my happy home.................. 196
Jesu, lover of my soul...................... 104
Jesu, my Lord, my God, my All............ 91
Jesu, name all names above................. 85
Jesu! the very thought of Thee.............. 87
Jesus, I love Thee,—not because............ 98
Jesus, I love Thy charming name............ 96
Jesus, I my cross have taken................ 83
Jesus' name shall ever be................... 107
Jesus shall reign where'er the sun........... 175
Jesus, still lead on......................... 94
Jesus, Thy Blood and Righteousness......... 63
Jesus, Thy boundless love to me............ 97
Just as I am,—without one plea............ 126

Lead, kindly Light, amid the encircling gloom.. 34
Leave God to order all thy ways............ 101
Let the world their virtue boast............. 151
Light of those whose dreary dwelling........ 174
Lo! He comes with clouds descending........ 184
Lo, on a narrow neck of land............... 15
Lord, it belongs not to my care............. 161
Lo, the feast is spread to-day!.............. 21
Love Divine, all loves excelling............. 106

My faith looks up to Thee.................. 146

Nearer, my God, to Thee................... 134
New every morning is the love.............. 35
No, no, it is not dying..................... 188

| | |
|---|---|
| Now I have found a friend................ | 130 |
| Now, my soul, thy voice upraising......... | 56 |
| | |
| O come, all ye faithful, triumphantly sing..... | 40 |
| O could I speak the matchless worth.......... | 152 |
| O day of rest and gladness.................. | 12 |
| O for a closer walk with God................ | 28 |
| O for a thousand tongues to sing............. | 154 |
| Of the Father's love begotten............ .... | 45 |
| O had I, my Saviour, the wings of a dove..... | 158 |
| Oh for a heart to praise my God!............. | 95 |
| Oh for the peace which floweth as a river..... | 127 |
| O Holy Saviour, Friend unseen!............. | 100 |
| O Jesus, we adore Thee..................... | 62 |
| O Lord, how happy should we be............ | 9 |
| O love divine, how sweet Thou art!.......... | 92 |
| O Master, it is good to be.................... | 27 |
| One there is, above all others................ | 111 |
| Onward, Christian soldiers................... | 168 |
| O Paradise, O Paradise...................... | 194 |
| O sacred Head! now wounded............... | 52 |
| Our God, our help in ages past............... | 2 |
| Our Lord is risen from the dead.............. | 77 |
| | |
| Praise, my soul, the King of Heaven.... ... | 24 |
| | |
| Rejoice, all ye believers...................... | 162 |
| Resting from His work to-day................ | 20 |
| Rest of the weary............................ | 114 |
| Rise, my soul, and stretch thy wings.......... | 29 |
| Rock of ages, cleft for me.................... | 129 |
| | |
| Safely, through another week................ | 14 |
| Saviour! when, in dust, to Thee.............. | 119 |
| See, the Conqueror mounts in triumph........ | 73 |
| Since o'er Thy footstool here below.......... | 33 |

## Index to first Lines.

| | |
|---|---|
| Softly now the light of day | 165 |
| Son of God, to Thee I cry | 80 |
| Star of peace, to wanderers weary | 164 |
| Still thy sorrow, Magdalena! | 72 |
| Sun of my soul, Thou Saviour dear | 159 |
| Sweet is the work, my God, my King | 23 |
| Sweet the moments, rich in blessing | 65 |
| | |
| Ten thousand times ten thousand | 197 |
| That mystic word of Thine, O sovereign Lord | 162 |
| The Head that once was crowned with thorns | 79 |
| The morning purples all the sky | 66 |
| There is a blessèd home | 189 |
| There is a fountain filled with blood | 59 |
| There is a land of pure delight | 193 |
| The Royal Banners forward go | 57 |
| The Saviour! O, what endless charms | 109 |
| The voice of free grace cries | 16 |
| The world is very evil | 200 |
| Thou art gone to the grave | 180 |
| Thou art my hiding place, O Lord | 103 |
| 'Tis the day of Resurrection | 70 |
| To Him, who for our sins was slain | 69 |
| Tossed with rough winds, and faint with fear | 137 |
| Trustingly, trustingly | 142 |
| | |
| Watchman! tell us of the night | 173 |
| We were not with the faithful few | 82 |
| What various hindrances we meet | 17 |
| When across the heart deep waves of sorrow | 136 |
| When all Thy mercies, O my God | 4 |
| When gathering clouds around I view | 120 |
| When I can read my title clear | 35 |
| When I survey the wondrous cross | 51 |
| When languor and disease invade | 179 |

When through the torn sail .................. 117
While Thee I seek, protecting Power ......... 22
While with ceaseless course the sun .......... 164
Who are these in bright array ............... 198
With broken heart and contrite sigh ......... 10
With tearful eyes I look around ............. 132

Ye golden lamps of heaven, farewell ......... 181

www.ingramcontent.com/pod-product-compliance
Lightning Source LLC
Chambersburg PA
CBHW021831230426
43669CB00008B/935